GRADES 1-6

Gospel Light's

BIG BOOK
OF BIBLE
LESSONS FOR
CRAFTY KIDS

Crafts and games bring lessons to life
Topics that build children's faith
Take-home pages to keep parents involved

Reproducible!

CD-ROM INCLUDED

WELCOME

Nothing is impossible with God! Luke 1:37

FORGIVE

Amy B. Pitcher

Gospel Light

Guidelines for Photocopying Pages

Permission to make photocopies of or to reproduce by any other mechanical or electronic means in whole or in part any designated* page, illustration or activity in this book is granted only to the original purchaser and is intended for noncommercial use within a church or other Christian organization. None of the material in this book may be reproduced for any commercial promotion, advertising or sale of a product or service. Sharing of the material in this book with other churches or organizations not owned or controlled by the original purchaser is also prohibited. All rights reserved.

*Pages with the following notation can be legally reproduced:

© 2007 Gospel Light. Permission to photocopy granted to original purchaser only.
The Big Book of Bible Lessons for Crafty Kids

Editorial Staff

Founder, Dr. Henrietta Mears • **Publisher,** William T. Greig • **Senior Consulting Publisher**, Dr. Elmer L. Towns • **Senior Managing Editor,** Sheryl Haystead • **Senior Consulting Editor,** Wesley Haystead, M.S.Ed. • **Senior Editor,** Biblical and Theological Issues, Bayard Taylor, M.Div. • **Associate Editor,** Veronica Neal • **Art Director,** Samantha A. Hsu • **Designer,** Christina Renée Sharp

Scripture quotations are taken from the Holy Bible, *New International Version*®. Copyright © 1973, 1978, 1984 by International Bible Society. Used by permission of Zondervan Publishing House. All rights reserved.

How to Use This Book

If you are the children's pastor,

1. Read "Introduction" on pages 6-7 to get an overview of *The Big Book of Bible Lessons for Crafty Kids.*

2. If *The Big Book of Bible Lessons for Crafty Kids* will be used as a separate children's program, you may want to recruit a coordinator several months before the program begins. Provide the coordinator with this book and plan regular check-ins with him or her. Be available for practical support and encouragement.

3. If teachers will use these lessons to supplement an existing curriculum, provide them with copies of each lesson.

If you are the coordinator,

1. Read "Introduction" on pages 6-7 to get an overview of *The Big Book of Bible Lessons for Crafty Kids.*

2. In conjunction with the children's pastor, recruit the appropriate number of small group leaders needed. (One adult for every small group of no more than 10 children is recommended.)

3. Use a calendar to plan when each lesson will be taught. (Note: The lessons follow a typical calendar year, but may be used in any order.)

4. Prepare ahead of time the materials needed for the craft and game activities. For crafts, in addition to the supplies listed with each activity, include basics such as rulers for measuring and newspapers or plastic tablecloths to cover work surfaces. (You may wish to recruit a supply coordinator to collect and distribute materials.)

5. Make a copy of each lesson's Faith Builders at Home page to distribute to parents of children at the conclusion of each lesson. These pages may also be downloaded from the CD-ROM in this book and e-mailed to parents.

If you are a teacher or small-group leader,

1. Read "Introduction" on pages 6-7 to get an overview of *The Big Book of Bible Lessons for Crafty Kids.*

2. Read the following articles: "Keep the Kids Talking!" and "Leading a Child to Christ" on pages 8 and 10.

3. Prepare and lead lessons to supplement your existing curriculum, or as assigned by program coordinator.

Big Book of Bible Lessons for Crafty Kids

Contents

Introduction

Children love to be active participants in their own learning process. The more they can get their hands into the lessons they are taught and creatively express themselves, the more exciting learning becomes. This is when the lessons they learn come to life and biblical values become a part of who they are.

That is why this book is designed to give elementary age children the opportunity to put their fingerprints all over the lessons. Children will hear biblical principles, talk about how the principles apply to their lives, express their creativity through crafty activities and have fun playing games that reinforce the Bible truth of the lesson.

The lessons in this book are designed to be used once a week with children in small groups. It is best if each small group consists of no more than 8 to 10 children and a

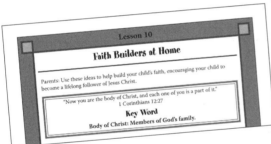

leader. The lessons can be used in second-hour programs, mid-week programs, after-school clubs, home churches, Christian schools and more. The topical lessons loosely coordinate with a typical calendar year, including lessons for several major holidays. However, you may use the lessons in any order you wish.

A special feature of each lesson is a parent connection page. Each Faith Builders at Home page includes the lesson Bible verse, the definition of the key word and three activity ideas that parents can use at home to build their child's faith in Jesus Christ. Designed for busy families, the activities offer parents an opportunity to be the spiritual teachers of their children. These pages can be distributed as take-home pages at the end of each lesson, or downloaded from the CD-ROM and e-mailed to parents.

Preparation Instructions

For a children's sermon. Photocopy the first page of each lesson to use as the text for a children's sermon during an adult worship time.

For a small-group lesson at church, at home, or for children whose parents are in a home study group. Photocopy the first page of each lesson for a small group leader

Introduction (continued)

or parent to use in leading children in Bible study and prayer. In addition, if time permits, consider leading children in the craft activity found on the second page of each lesson.

For the basis of a complete session at church. Photocopy the first three pages of each lesson. Distribute to small group leaders, craft and game leaders.

Customize Lessons for Your Group

As you plan and prepare to use the materials in this book, think about how best to adapt specific activities to your particular group's needs. Adapt games as needed to fit both your facility and the ages and abilities of your students. Modify crafts for younger children by simplifying the craft materials, or preparing materials ahead of time. This advance planning will ensure that all children can participate successfully.

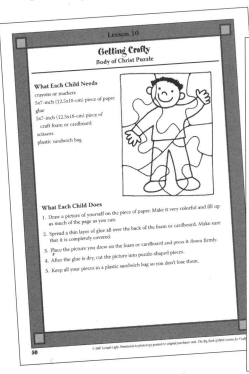

Keep the Kids Talking!

Children like to speak their minds! The challenge is to keep the discussion focused on the lesson, to involve all children and to prevent distracting chatter. Children's learning will be much more effective when they are involved in the process of learning through discovery and discussion rather than through sitting and listening.

Good Preparation

Write good questions before class. Good discussions occur when the teacher knows what questions to ask. Study the class material thoroughly (even if it's a familiar Bible verse or story) and think through the discussion questions provided in your curriculum. Think of additional questions to ask as well. Avoid questions with obvious one-word answers. Discussion grows out of questions that ask for opinions, ideas, reactions, etc., not just repeating factual answers. (This means you must begin preparation well before Sunday morning!)

Minimize distractions. Children are naturally curious and are interested in everything that goes on—whether it's the lesson activity at hand or not! Evaluate the distractions in your classroom by asking the following questions: Is there noise in the classroom from the choir warming up next door? Are people walking through the hallway? Are there toys or items scattered around the classroom that the children will want to play with? Are cell phones ringing? Do parents arrive long before the class ends and stand around outside the room?

Then consider these solutions: If outside noise is a problem, play a music CD or cassette as background to cover outside noise.

Toy shelves can be turned to face the wall to help children avoid the temptation of playing with the toys. Arrange chairs so children are faced away from distractions. Remind teachers (and children!) before class begins to turn off cell phones. Keep in mind, however, that your reaction to distractions is the biggest factor. If you respond in a matter-of-fact manner, children will, also.

Limit the discussion. Children are not able to remain interested during long times of discussion. Children's physical requirements for movement need to be met. It's better to end the discussion time before children grow restless. Most discussions should be tied to some physical activity, either as an introduction to the activity, as a break during the activity or as a summary after the activity.

Involve everyone. Try to involve all children in a discussion. Start by asking several easy, low-threat questions that all children are capable of answering. Seek to involve the potentially disruptive child right at the start. Children are less likely to be disruptive when they're occupied. If a child looks restless, call him or her by name and ask a question. Also ask questions of children who have been quiet. Be sure not to ask a difficult question they may not know. One reason children may not participate is that they feel they don't know the answer and don't want to be embarrassed in front of their peers.

Handling Interruptions

Get back on track. Despite the best plans, a discussion may veer off course. First, determine if the new topic is valid. Perhaps one child is overly focused on a small detail

Keep the Kids Talking! (continued)

(such as how Joshua could make the sun stand still when in reality Earth moves) but the rest of the class is not interested. Acknowledge that the new topic is interesting and can be discussed at another time, and then return to the original topic. Restate the last question and if children do not respond, try another question.

If a child deliberately wants to get off the topic, use humor to return to the topic. If the children digress because they don't understand the topic or the question, use a simpler question or take time to explain the topic.

Discussion off the topic is not always cause for alarm. Sometimes a child needs to discuss a topic not on the agenda or finds an unexplored point in the topic. If the new topic will help children apply Bible truth to everyday life and will benefit the entire class, stay with it. If a child needs to discuss a special need, such as a death in the family, make time at the end of the activity for the class to offer support and prayer.

Go with the flow. Interruptions will happen. If the interruption is minor and the children are not unduly distracted, then ignore it and continue. Some interruptions require the teacher to stop and take care of matters: a child needs to leave early, an adult arrives to make an announcement or the air conditioner needs to be adjusted. Try to get the class back on track. If the class has grown too distracted, move on to another activity.

Be prepared for silence. Sometimes children will respond to a question with silence. This can be good if the children are pondering a deep question. It can be fatal if this is due to lack of understanding, embarrassment or boredom.

Give children a few seconds to think about the question. Ask for a visual signal (thumb up, fist on chin, etc.) when students think they may have at least part of the answer. Rephrase the question in case the first question was not understood. If children still are unable to answer, you might share the answer you would give and then move on to another question.

Some children may feel uncomfortable speaking in front of a large class. Divide the children into small groups of six or fewer in which to discuss the answers. Provide to each group large sheets of paper on which to write their answers. Then a volunteer from each group shares the replies with the whole class. Small groups are also good for discussing sensitive or personal topics, perhaps occasionally forming all-boy and all-girl small groups.

Sometimes children do not respond when the questions are too easy (Who are Jesus' parents?), too obvious (Does God want us to help our neighbors?), too personal (What sins have you committed this week?) or too difficult (According to legend, what are the names of the three wise men?). After class, revise the questions that failed to get a good response and use the improvements as a model for writing good questions for the next class.

Sometimes children will give the answer they think the teacher wants to hear. Write open-ended questions that are more challenging: How would you feel if you had been a shepherd who was off-duty the night the angels appeared? What do you think the blind man did after Jesus healed him? How can you defend your friend from a bully?

Leading A Child to Christ

Many adult Christians look back to their elementary years as the time when they accepted Christ as Savior. Not only are children able to understand the difference between right and wrong and their own personal need of forgiveness, but they are also growing in their ability to understand Jesus' death and resurrection as the means by which God provides salvation. In addition, children at this age are capable of growing in their faith through prayer, Bible reading, worship and service.

However, children (particularly those in early elementary grades) can still be limited in their understanding and may be immature in following through on their intentions and commitments. They need thoughtful, patient guidance in coming to know Christ personally and continuing to grow in Him.

1. Pray.

Ask God to prepare the children in your class to receive the good news about Jesus and prepare you to effectively communicate with them.

2. Present the Good News.

Use words and phrases that children understand. Avoid symbolism that will confuse these literal-minded thinkers. Discuss these points slowly enough to allow time for thinking and comprehending.

a. "God wants you to become His child. Do you know why God wants you in His family?" (See 1 John 3:1.)

b. "You and all the people in the world have done wrong things. The Bible word for doing wrong is 'sin.' What do you think the Bible says should happen to us when we sin?" (See Romans 6:23.)

c. "God loves you so much, He sent His Son to die on the cross for your sin. Because Jesus never sinned, He is the only one who can take the punishment for your sin. On the third day after Jesus died, God brought Him back to life." (See 1 Corinthians 15:3-4; 1 John 4:14.)

d. "Are you sorry for your sin? Tell God that you are. Do you believe Jesus died to take the punishment for your sin and that He is alive today? If you tell God you are sorry for your sin and tell Him you do believe and accept Jesus' death to take away your sin—God forgives all your sin." (See 1 John 1:9.)

e. "The Bible says that when you believe in Jesus, God's Son, you receive God's gift of eternal life. This gift makes you a child of God. This means God is with you now and forever." (See John 1:13.)

As you give children many opportunities to think about what it means to be a Christian, expose them to a variety of lessons and descriptions of the meaning of salvation to aid their understanding.

3. Talk personally with the child.

Talking about salvation one-on-one creates opportunity to ask and answer questions. Ask questions that move the child

Leading A Child to Christ (continued)

beyond simple yes or no answers or recitation of memorized information. Ask what-do-you-think? kinds of questions such as:

"Why do you think it's important to . . . ?"

"What are some things you really like about Jesus?"

"Why do you think that Jesus had to die because of wrong things you and I have done?"

"What difference do you think it makes for a person to be forgiven?"

Answers to these open-ended questions will help you discern how much the child does or does not understand.

4. Offer opportunities without pressure.

Children are vulnerable to being manipulated by adults. A good way to guard against coercing a child's response is to simply pause periodically and ask, "Would you like to hear more about this now or at another time?" Lovingly accepting the child, even when he or she is not fully interested in pursuing the matter, is crucial in building and maintaining relationship that will yield more opportunities to talk about becoming part of God's family.

5. Give time to think and pray.

There is great value in encouraging a child to think and pray about what you have said before making a response. Also allow moments for quiet thinking about questions you ask.

6. Respect the child's response.

Whether or not a child declares faith in Jesus Christ, adults need to accept the child's action. There is also a need to realize that a child's initial responses to Jesus are just the beginning of a lifelong process of growing in the faith.

7. Guide the child in further growth.

Here are three important parts in the nurturing process:

a. Talk regularly about your relationship with God. As you talk about your relationship, the child will begin to feel that it's OK to talk about such things. Then you can comfortably ask the child to share his or her thoughts and feelings, and encourage the child to ask questions of you.

b. Prepare the child to deal with doubts. Emphasize that certainty about salvation is not dependent on our feelings or doing enough good deeds. Show the child verses in God's Word that clearly declare that salvation comes by grace through faith (i.e., John 1:12; Ephesians 2:8-9; Hebrews 11:6; 1 John 5:11).

c. Teach the child to confess all sin. "Confess" means "to admit" or "to agree." Confessing sins means agreeing with God that we really have sinned. Assure the child that confession always results in forgiveness (see 1 John 1:9).

Starting Out Right

Lesson 1
A New Creation

"Therefore, if anyone is in Christ, he is a new creation; the old has gone, the new has come!" 2 Corinthians 5:17

Key Word

Change: To become different.

Opening Up

When have you dressed up in a costume? What did you dress up as?

Did dressing up change who you were? Why or why not? Invite children to respond.

Checking Out God's Word

Frogs go through major changes in their lives that are permanent.

■ How do frogs look when they are babies compared to when they grow up?

Today we are going to talk about how we can make permanent changes in our lives too. Read 2 Corinthians 5:17 aloud.

■ What does the verse say makes a person a new creation?

■ What do you think it means to be in Christ?

We don't exactly change our appearances like frogs do. When frogs become new creations, their bodies change from tiny tadpoles to full grown frogs. When we become new creations like the Bible says, God helps us to change our way of thinking and the way we behave. He helps us show our love for Him and others.

The next part of the verse says "the old has gone." These words remind us that even though everyone does things that are wrong, we can ask for God's forgiveness when we do wrong things. When God forgives our sins, we can ask His help to live in the new ways God wants us to live.

■ What kinds of things would you like to change to show your love for God and others?

Talking to God

We can ask God to change the way we think and act. That is how we become new creations. We don't have to think about the old things we've done anymore. We can stay focused on the new ways that God wants us to live and act. Let's pray and ask God to help us become new creations for Him. Pick the person who is wearing the most green to pray today. Lead children in prayer.

Getting Crafty
Froggy Plant Stick

What Each Child Needs

2¹/₂-inch (6.5-cm) styrofoam ball

butter knife

paintbrush

green acrylic paint

red acrylic paint

scissors

6-inch (15-cm) square of green craft foam

4-inch (10-cm) square white or colored
    craft foam

permanent marker

wooden skewer

¹/₄-inch (.6-cm) wiggly eyes

craft glue

thumb tacks

What Each Child Does

1. With an adult's help, begin by cutting a mouth in the styrofoam ball with the butter knife. Then paint the ball green, and the inside of the mouth red. Set it aside to dry.

2. Using the green craft foam, cut out back legs and front legs for the frog. Out of the white craft foam, cut out a flag in the desired shape.

3. Using a permanent marker, write "I'm a new creation!" on the flag. Poke the skewer through the flag twice and slide it into place with the point facing down.

4. By now the body should be dry. Glue on two wiggly eyes, and glue on the front legs and back legs. Use a thumb tack to hold the legs in place until they dry.

5. For the final assembly, poke the blunt end of the skewer into the stomach of the frog. Take home the frog and stick it in your favorite houseplant.

Getting Active

What You Need

blindfold

What You Do

1. Play a game like Marco Polo. Ask a child to stand to one side of the playing area.

2. Blindfold the child.

3. Children quietly position themselves in random places around the playing area. Blindfolded child begins to call "I am. . . ." Rest of students answer "a new creation." Blindfolded child moves toward children by listening to their voices. As he or she continues calling "I am . . . ," children around the room respond each time. Depending on the size of your playing area, the children who respond to the blindfolded child may stay frozen in one spot or may move around as they respond.

4. When the blindfolded child finds or tags another child, that child (or a child who hasn't had a turn yet) is blindfolded for the next round. Continue game as time permits.

Faith Builders at Home

Parents: Use these ideas to help build your child's faith, encouraging your child to become a lifelong follower of Jesus Christ.

"Therefore, if anyone is in Christ, he is a new creation; the old has gone, the new has come!" 2 Corinthians 5:17

Key Word

Change: To become different.

Steppin' Out

If you've never tried it before, consider looking for tadpoles in a nearby stream or lake. If you find a tadpole, keep it in clean water with some lettuce leaves and watch as it transforms into a frog. Don't forget to return it to its natural habitat when it can hop! (Hint: If tadpoles are scarce in your area, try the pet shop or the Internet.)

Quick Pick

Print the words of 2 Corinthians 5:17 on a sheet of paper. Give each family member a different color crayon or marker. Each person chooses a word in the verse he or she thinks is most important, circles it and tells why he or she chose the word.

Fun at Home

Give everyone three minutes to collect recyclables (aluminum cans, bottles, shoe boxes, etc.). Set out tape, string, scissors and foil. Have your family members work together to create something new (an invention, a statue, a game, etc.) using the collected items. Talk about the new ways God wants us to live and act.

Starting Out Right

Lesson 2
Molded by God

"O Lord, you are our Father. We are the clay, you are the potter; we are all the work of your hand." Isaiah 64:8

Key Word

Creation: Bringing something new into the world.

Opening Up

Think about something you have made that you really love or are really proud of. It could be a drawing, building project, craft, or anything that you created. Invite children to respond.

Checking Out God's Word

■ **How did you know how to create your project?**

You knew how to create your project because you were the creator. The creator knows best when putting together a creation. God knew exactly how to create you! He helped you grow in your mom's belly. He didn't need to ask you how to do it. Read Isaiah 64:8 aloud.

■ **Who does the verse say is the "clay"? The "potter"?**

God is like a potter. A potter is someone who creates things from clay. When we love and obey God, we are like clay that can be molded by the potter. God is able to mold us into what He wants us to be. We can ask God to create us into the people He wants us to be.

■ **Why do you think it's better to let God mold our lives instead of doing it ourselves?**

■ **What are some things that we can do to allow God to mold our lives?**

Talking to God

As we pray today, let's hold our hands with our palms facing up. When we sit like this, it shows God that we are open to His ways and that we want Him to mold us like a potter. Repeat this prayer after me. Lead children in prayer. Father God, thank You for creating me and wanting what is best for me. Please mold me into the person that You want me to be. In Jesus' name, amen.

Getting Crafty
Homemade Play Dough

What Each Child Needs

fist-sized lump of play dough

cookie sheet

oven

acrylic paint

paintbrush

optional—food coloring

To make play dough, you need:
3 cups (710 ml) of flour
2 tablespoons (30 ml) of oil
1 1/2 cups (360 ml) of water
large bowl
Mix flour, oil and water in a large bowl. The consistency should be thick, but not crumbly. You can add more flour or water if necessary.

What Each Child Does

1. Use the play dough to mold a small person that resembles you. With an adult's help, place your creation on an ungreased cookie sheet and bake for about 1 hour at 250 degrees.

2. Let the dough cool completely and then paint with acrylic paints. (Optional: If time is limited, consider forming the play dough at one session, baking it later, and painting it at the next session, or instead of baking and painting, divide the clay into parts and color the parts different colors with food coloring.)

Getting Active

What You Need

Bibles

slips of paper

marker

balloons

garbage bag

What You Do

1. Print one to three words from Isaiah 64:8 on separate slips of paper, making one paper for each child. Blow up balloons, inserting one rolled slip of paper into each balloon before tying. Put balloons in a garbage bag.

2. Children choose balloons, pop them and find papers inside.

3. Children read the verse in the Bibles and arrange slips of paper in order.

The Big Book of Bible Lessons for Crafty Kids

Faith Builders at Home

Parents: Use these ideas to help build your child's faith, encouraging your child to become a lifelong follower of Jesus Christ.

"O Lord, you are our Father. We are the clay, you are the potter; we are all the work of your hand." Isaiah 64:8

Key Word

Creation: Bringing something new into the world.

Fun at Home

Make homemade mini pizzas with your children this week. (Optional: Use English muffins for mini pizza crust.) Allow them to create their own special pizzas with various toppings. Compare how being the pizza maker who makes pizzas is similar to how God creates us.

Quick Pick

Set aside a few minutes for a family prayer time this week. In your prayer, ask family members to thank God for creating them and tell Him three things that they like about themselves.

Steppin' Out

Take a creation walk around your neighborhood. Look at the trees, insects, birds and plants. Talk about how God is the creator of every living thing.

Starting Out Right

Lesson 3
Attitude Check

"Your attitude should be the same as that of Christ Jesus."
Philippians 2:5

Key Word

Attitude: A feeling that affects the way you talk and act.

Opening Up

How might you act and talk when you feel sad? Angry? Thankful? Frustrated? Embarrassed? Happy? Invite children to respond.

Checking Out God's Word

Our attitude is shown in the things we say and do. When we feel angry, we may say mean things or cross our arms in front of our chest to show others we're angry. The Bible has something important to say about our attitudes. Have a child read Philippians 2:4-8 aloud.

■ In verse 5, who does the Bible say our attitudes should be like?

■ If you were to describe Jesus' attitude in your own words, what would you say?

Jesus is the example of what kind of attitude we should have. Jesus showed that He had a humble attitude. When someone is humble, he or she thinks of others first and does not brag.

■ In verse 8, what did Jesus do to show He was humble?

Jesus was willing to die on a cross! He was concerned about others more than Himself and He showed how much He loved them. When we remember Jesus' love, it reminds us to be humble and be concerned about the needs of others.

■ What kinds of things make it hard for a kid your age to have an attitude like Jesus and be concerned about others?

■ When can you act or talk to show that your attitude is like Jesus?

Talking to God

God understands that it can be hard for us to think about the needs of others. But we can always ask for His help. Lead children in prayer. **Thank Jesus for His love and humble attitude. Ask for God's help in following Jesus' example.** (Optional: Everyone finds a partner. Kids share with his or her partner a way in which they would like to show a humble attitude. Kids take turns praying for each other and thanking Jesus for the humble attitude He showed.

The Big Book of Bible Lessons for Crafty Kids

Getting Crafty

Attitude Check Reminder Magnet

What Each Child Needs

8x11-inch (20.5x28-cm) piece of white
  craft foam

pencil

scissors

colored craft foam pieces

permanent marker

craft glue

4 small magnets

optional—precut craft foam letters

What Each Child Does

1. Using a pencil, draw the shape of a large check mark on the white craft foam. Cut out this shape.

2. Using the permanent marker, write the word "Attitude" on the colored craft foam. Cut out the letters of the word. (Optional: Use precut letters.)

3. Glue the letters onto the white check mark.

4. Turn over the project and glue the magnets around the edges.

5. Take home the attitude check magnet and keep it on the refrigerator as a reminder of what your attitude should be.

Getting Active

What You Need

one tube sock for each pair of children

What You Do

1. **Let's play a game where we practice being concerned for others. Children form pairs.** (Optional: Have children who are similar in height form pairs.) Pairs stand on one side of the playing area.

2. Give each pair a tube sock. Partners hold sock between them, each with one hand on the sock. Pairs practice stepping over the sock, one foot at a time, without letting go of the sock.

3. To begin game, children stand at one side of the playing area. At your signal, one child in the pair says "After you," and his or her partner takes a step, putting one foot and then the other over the sock. Then the partner who stepped says "After you," and the other partner takes a turn. Children continue in this matter, moving across the playing area and back. Play several more rounds if time permits.

Faith Builders at Home

Parents: Use these ideas to help build your child's faith, encouraging your child to become a lifelong follower of Jesus Christ.

"Your attitude should be the same as that of Christ Jesus."
Philippians 2:5

Key Word

Attitude: A feeling that affects the way you talk and act.

Fun at Home

Play a family game of Charades. Talk about actions that show the type of attitude we should have toward others (kind, generous, peaceful, helpful, etc.). Then take turns choosing an action and acting it out for others to guess.

Quick Pick

Collect a beanbag or ball. Read Galatians 5:22-23 for a list of attitudes. Toss the beanbag or ball to each other. Each time someone catches the beanbag or ball, he or she calls out one of the attitudes and tells a way to show it.

Steppin' Out

Buy a set of magnetic refrigerator letters and spell out on your refrigerator different attitudes that show love for God and others.

Starting Out Right

Lesson 4
A Pure Heart

"Create in me a pure heart, O God, and renew a steadfast spirit within me."
Psalm 51:10

Key Word

Pure: To be free from sin.

Opening Up

Because of God's love and forgiveness, we can have a fresh start at any moment! New Year's Day is a time when most people stop to think about making a fresh start. **What is something you'd like to be different this year?** Invite children to tell ideas.

Checking Out God's Word

Have a child read Psalm 51:10 aloud.

■ **What do you think the word "pure" means?**

■ **What are some things that are pure?**

The word "pure" means to be free from sin. We can ask God to help us be pure and do the right thing. When we do wrong things, we can ask God to forgive us and give us a pure heart to do the right things.

■ **What do you think the phrase "renew a steadfast spirit within me" means?**

Another word for "steadfast" is "faithful." The author of the verse is asking God to help him to stay faithful to God. If we stay faithful to God, we will do our best not to do wrong things.

Talking to God

Our God is so great, and He wants to make our hearts pure! We can ask Him to help us. Let's take some time to tell God that we are sorry for the wrong things we have done and ask for His forgiveness. Let's ask Him to help us have pure hearts and to do the right things. Lead children in prayer allowing some brief time for children to pray silently.

Getting Crafty
Heart Plaque

What Each Child Needs

12x12-inch (30.5x30.5-cm) piece of wood at least $^1/_2$ inch (1.3 cm) thick

pencil

hammer

12 to 15 nails at least 1 inch
    (2.5 cm) long

3 yards (91 cm) long of yarn or
    embroidery thread

permanent marker

scissors

optional—acrylic paint,
    paint brush

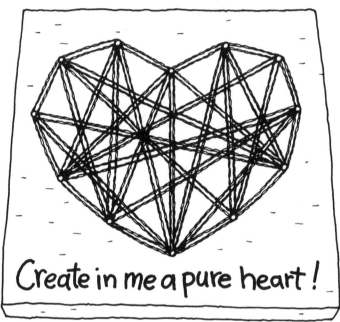

Create in me a pure heart!

What Each Child Does

1. (Optional: Paint the block of wood before you begin the project.) Using a pencil, draw a large heart shape on the block of wood. Have an adult help you pound nails about $^1/_4$ inch (.6 cm) into the wood along the pencil line heart, leaving about $1^1/_2$ inches (4 cm) in between each nail.

2. Choose a starting nail and tie the end of the yarn tightly to the nail. Begin threading the yarn to other nails to create a pattern. As you reach each new nail, wrap the yarn tightly around the nail before moving on to the next one. Continue going back and forth between nails until you've run out of room on the nails or you've run out of yarn.

3. When you are finished with your pattern, tie the end of the yarn tightly to one of the nails.

4. Using a permanent marker, write "Create in me a pure heart!" under or around the yarn pattern.

Getting Active

What You Need

Bibles

one chair for each child

index cards

marker

Post-it Notes

children's music CD and player

What You Do

1. Place chairs in a large circle facing inward. Print "Create in me a pure heart, O God, and renew a steadfast spirit within me" on index cards, one word on each card. Mix up the cards. Make an X on one Post-it Note. Stick a Post-it Note, including the one with the X, on the back of each chair.

2. As you play music, children walk around the inside of the circle of chairs. Stop the music after a few moments. Each child sits in a chair.

3. Children look over the backs of their chairs to locate the chair with the X on it. Give child sitting in the marked chair a verse card. Child places card on the floor in the middle of the circle.

4. Move Post-it Notes to different chairs so that the note with an X is on the back of a different chair. Then repeat play. When music stops, children sit down and check for the X. Child in marked chair gets a second verse card and decides whether it should be placed before or after the first card. Continue play until all verse cards are placed in the right order. Children refer to Psalm 51:10 for correct order if needed.

Faith Builders at Home

Parents: Use these ideas to help build your child's faith, encouraging your child to become a lifelong follower of Jesus Christ.

"Create in me a pure heart, O God, and renew a steadfast spirit within me."
Psalm 51:10

Key Word

Pure: To be free from sin.

Fun at Home

Place a cup of water in front of each family member on a table. Give each family member a sheet of paper and a pencil. Have each person write a list of ways they use pure water every day. Call time after one minute. Read lists aloud and talk about how God gives us a pure heart to love and obey Him.

Quick Pick

Read more of David's prayer in Psalm 51:1-12 and answer the following question, "What do you learn about God from these verses?"

Steppin' Out

Participate in a pure water experiment! Gather two clean jars with lids, soil, a large spoon, clean sand, an 8-inch (20.5-cm) square of cheesecloth or cotton fabric and a rubber band. Fill one jar halfway with water. Add some soil to the jar with water. Put the lid on tightly. Shake the jar to make muddy water. Lay the cloth over the opening of the second jar, letting the cloth sag down into the opening. Place rubber band around the cloth and jar. Spoon the sand onto the cloth. Pour the muddy water slowly through the sand. Observe how the water in the second jar looks. Ask children, "Why do you think the water looks this way?"

Starting Out Right

Lesson 5
Loving God

> "This is love for God: to obey his commands."
> 1 John 5:3

Key Word

Obey: To follow commands or guidance.

Opening Up

How do you know that someone loves you? How do you show the important people in your life that you love them? Invite children to respond.

Checking Out God's Word

Today our lesson is about showing love to God. The Bible tells us exactly how we can show love to God. Have a child read 1 John 5:3 aloud. (Optional: Have the child with the fewest letters in his or her name read aloud.)

■ **What can we do to show love to God?**

■ **Why do you think that obeying God shows how much we love Him?**

Let's make a list of commands you think God wants us to obey. Give sheet of paper and pencil to each child. Allow a few moments for children to write. (Optional: Children tell commands. Write them on one large sheet of paper.) **Let's talk about some of the commands you have on your lists.** Invite children to tell ideas.

■ **When might it be hard for a kid your age to obey God's commands?**

It can be hard to obey God's commands all the time. It's good to know that we can ask for God's help to obey Him. When we obey God's commands, we are showing Him that we love Him. Let's look again at the commands you listed.

■ **Which command on your list do you want to obey more now than you have in the past?**

Talking to God

Let's take a few moments for a silent prayer. During your silent prayer, tell God how much you love Him. Then speak to Him about a command on your list that you want to obey. Ask for His help to obey that command. Lead children in prayer.

Getting Crafty
Heart Hanger

What Each Child Needs

Bible

pencil

2 8x11-inch (20.5x28-cm) sheets of pink
   or other light-colored craft foam

scissors

permanent marker

stapler

cotton balls or batting

1 pipe cleaner

6 inches (15 cm) of ribbon

What Each Child Does

1. Using a pencil, draw a large heart shape on one sheet of craft foam. Cut out the heart and trace around it on the other sheet of craft foam. Cut out the second heart.

2. On one heart, use a permanent marker to write the words of 1 John 5:3. Place hearts back-to-back.

3. Have an adult help you staple around the edges of the hearts, leaving an opening to stuff the cotton in. After you have filled the heart with cotton, staple the opening closed.

4. To make the handle, poke one end of the pipe cleaner through the top edge of the heart and twist it so it won't come out of the hole. Loop the pipe cleaner over and poke it through the heart again, forming a rainbow shape over the top of the heart. Twist the end to secure it in place.

5. Tie a bow on the pipe cleaner with the ribbon for extra decoration.

Getting Active

What You Need

construction paper

markers

masking tape

children's music CD and player

What You Do

1. Print the letters O, B, E, Y, G, O and D on separate sheets of construction paper. Tape the papers to the floor in a large circle.

2. Each child stands near one of the letters. (More than one child may stand near any letter.) As you play the music, children move to stand by different letters. Stop the music. Call out any one of the letters. The children standing near the letter each tell a situation in which kids their age can obey God's commands. (Note: There are two O's in phrase. Have each child standing next to the same letters tell a situation in which kids their age can obey God's commands.)

3. Continue to play game as time permits.

Faith Builders at Home

Parents: Use these ideas to help build your child's faith, encouraging your child to become a lifelong follower of Jesus Christ.

> "This is love for God: to obey his commands."
> 1 John 5:3
>
> ## Key Word
>
> **Obey: To follow commands or guidance.**

Quick Pick

One of God's commands is that children obey their parents. Using your Bible, read Colossians 3:20 aloud. Let your children know that even grown-ups have to obey others. Tell an example of a time when you obeyed someone. Then, ask your children, "Why would God want children to obey their parents? What would happen if no one obeyed anyone?" Discuss answers.

Steppin' Out

Outside on the front lawn or at a park, have your family stand in a circle. Each family member takes a turn going to the middle of the circle, spinning around several times with eyes closed and one hand pointing out. After spinning, child opens eyes. The person to whom child is pointing tells one way to obey God's commands.

Fun at Home

Play a game of Simon Says except use the names of family members to give commands. For example, say "(Jenna) says touch your ears." At the end of the game, talk about how God can help us to obey His commands.

Starting Out Right

Lesson 6
Loving Each Other (Valentine's Day)

> "Be devoted to one another in brotherly love. Honor one another above yourselves." Romans 12:10

Key Word

Honor: To show sincere respect for someone.

Opening Up

What are some things that you like to do with your friends? What are some things that you like to do with your family? Invite children to tell ideas.

Checking Out God's Word

Today we're going to talk about how we can honor and show love to people in our lives. Have a child read Romans 12:10 aloud.

■ **What command are we given in the first sentence of this verse?**

The first part of this verse tells us to be devoted to one another. To be devoted to someone means to faithfully care about the person. The verse then tells us to have brotherly love. When we become a part of God's family, it's like we are brothers and sisters. God wants us to treat one another with love and respect like we are brothers and sisters.

■ **What command are we given in the second sentence of this verse?**

To show honor to someone means to show sincere respect for him or her. Many times we learn to honor people like our parents and teachers. However, we can honor people of any age—even our brothers, sisters and friends!

■ **Do you think it's easy or hard to honor others? Why?**

■ **What are some ways that you can honor someone else at home? At church? At school? In your neighborhood?**

Talking to God

Lead children in prayer, asking His help to honor others. If appropriate, help children form pairs. **In your pairs, take turns praying for one another. Tell each other the name of someone you want to honor. Ask God to help your partner honor and show love to the person this week.**

Getting Crafty
Marble Valentines

What Each Child Needs

shallow box (big enough to lay 8^1/$_2$ x11-inch (21.5x28-cm) paper flat in the bottom of the box)

8^1/$_2$ x 11-inch (21.5x28-cm) white paper

3 to 5 marbles

acrylic paint (assorted colors)

pink, red or black card stock

pen, pencil or gel markers

scissors

glue stick

What Each Child Does

1. Lay a sheet of white paper flat in the bottom of the box. Put the marbles in the box and add a small squirt of three different colors of paint on the paper.

2. With an adult's help, gently tip the box so that the marbles roll to one side across the paint on the paper. Repeat this several times until the paper is covered in paint and you like the design you have created.

3. Take the paper out of the box and set it aside to dry. (Clean off the marbles if you are going to make another painting.)

4. Take a sheet of red, pink or black card stock and fold it in half to make a card. While your painting is drying, use a pen, pencil or gel markers to write a note to someone you know that you want to show love to. It can be a teacher, a family member or a friend.

5. When your paint is dry, cut out heart shapes from the painted paper. You can make one big heart or several small hearts—whatever you like! Use a glue stick to glue the hearts as desired onto the front of the card.

Getting Active

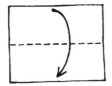

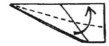

What You Need

Bibles

paper

markers

What You Do

1. Practice making two paper airplanes following the sketches above. Write the words of Romans 12:10 on each paper airplane. Give a marker to each child. Help children form a large circle.

2. Fly prepared airplanes to children. Each child unfolds and reads the Bible verse aloud and then writes down one way to honor and show love to someone. Children refold airplanes and fly them to other children.

3. Continue game as time permits. Add additional airplanes to game.

The Big Book of Bible Lessons for Crafty Kids

Faith Builders at Home

Parents: Use these ideas to help build your child's faith, encouraging your child to become a lifelong follower of Jesus Christ.

"Be devoted to one another in brotherly love. Honor one another above yourselves." Romans 12:10

Key Word

Honor: To show sincere respect for someone.

Steppin' Out

One day this week, have your family bake goodies (a cake, cookies, brownies, etc.) for another family on your block. Design a greeting card signed by all family members to present with your baked treats.

Fun at Home

Using paper and markers or crayons, have each family member draw a stick-figure comic strip showing a way to honor and show love to someone else. Put the comic strips together to create a comic book.

Quick Pick

Write each family member's name on a separate slip of paper. Place papers into a bag or basket. Each family member chooses one slip of paper. The name of the person on the slip of paper will be the person that he or she will honor for the rest of the day. If someone picks his or her own name, he or she will choose another slip of paper until they choose a name other than their own. Repeat each day of the week.

Starting Out Right

Lesson 7
Smile, God Loves You!

"This is love: not that we loved God, but that he loved us and sent his Son as an atoning sacrifice for our sins." 1 John 4:10

Key Word

Love: To show strong affection and concern for someone.

Opening Up

What is something that makes you smile? Why does it make you smile? Invite children to tell ideas.

Checking Out God's Word

Some people use the phrase "Smile, God loves you!" We may see this phrase on key chains and bumper stickers. Let's find out what the Bible says about why God's love can make us smile. Have a child read 1 John 4:10 aloud. (Optional: Have a child whose birthday is closest to Valentine's Day read aloud.)

■ In your own words, what does this verse say love is?

This verse tells us that God loved us before we loved Him. The reason we know that God loved us is because He sent His Son, Jesus, to die for the wrong things we have done.

■ Why do you think God loves us so much?

■ What else has God done to show His love for us?

God loves us and wants everyone to recognize that He sent Jesus to die for us. Sometimes people don't choose to recognize that God sent Jesus to die for us. But for those of us who do, God promises that we will live with Him forever!

Talking to God

Let's pray to God and thank Him for loving us so much. Lead children in prayer. Dear God, thank You for loving us so much. We love You because You first loved us. In Jesus' name, amen.

Getting Crafty
Smiley Face Door Hanger

What Each Child Needs

dry pasta in assorted colors and shapes

newspaper

black acrylic paint

paintbrush

12-inch (30.5-cm) yellow paper plate

black marker

single hole punch

18-inch (45.5-cm) piece of black ribbon or yarn

scissors

glue

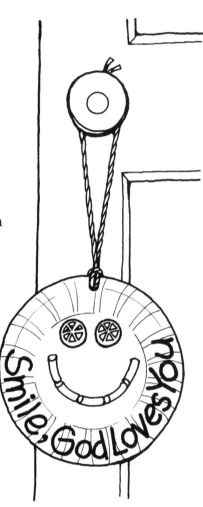

What Each Child Does

1. Decide which pasta shapes you want to use to create eyes and a mouth. Then set pasta shapes on newspaper and use the black paint to paint the pasta. (Optional: Instead of painting pasta, leave pasta its original assorted color.) Set it aside to dry.

2. With the black marker, write "Smile, God Loves You" around the edge of the paper plate. Punch one hole in the top of the plate. Cut and tie an 18-inch (45.5-cm) piece of ribbon or yarn through the hole to create a loop.

3. Glue the pasta into place and allow it to dry completely before hanging plate on a doorknob.

Getting Active

GOD'S LOVE

What You Need

string or yarn

scissors

stopwatch or watch with a second hand

What You Do

1. Cut string into varying lengths (at least two lengths for each student). Hide string in classroom or outdoor area.

2. Group children in two or more teams of four to five each.

3. At your signal, children look for and collect string, trying to find as many pieces as they can in 30 seconds.

4. After time is called, team members lay out end-to-end the pieces of string they have collected. Team who collected the longest length wins. Play additional rounds of this game as time permits. At the end of the game, teams use string to spell out the words "God's Love."

Faith Builders at Home

Parents: Use these ideas to help build your child's faith, encouraging your child to become a lifelong follower of Jesus Christ.

"This is love: not that we loved God, but that he loved us and sent his Son as an atoning sacrifice for our sins." 1 John 4:10

Key Word

Love: To show strong affection and concern for someone.

Quick Pick

Before a meal or at bedtime, each family member thanks God for one way God has shown love to him or her.

Fun at Home

Using strips of construction paper, tape and markers, make a love chain to remember God's love for your family. Each family member writes his or her name on several strips of paper. Tape strips together to form a paper chain. Loop each strip of paper together with a piece of tape. Hang your love chain in a window, on a door or in your car.

Steppin' Out

Visit your local garden store and buy some colorful flowers. As a love offering, offer to plant flowers in a neighbor's yard.

Starting Out Right

Lesson 8
A Caring Heart

"I tell you the truth, whatever you did for one of the least of these brothers of mine, you did for me." Matthew 25:40

Key Word

Care: To express genuine interest or concern.

Opening Up

How do you show that you care about someone or something? Invite children to tell ideas.

Checking Out God's Word

We care about many things around us. We love and care for our families, our friends and even our pets. The Bible tells us that it is good to care for others because God cares for us. Have a child read Matthew 25:35-40 aloud.

- **In verses 35 and 36, what are six examples of ways to show care for someone?**

- **When is a time you or someone you know has cared for someone in one of these ways?**

The Bible says that we can feed those who are hungry, give something to drink to those who are thirsty, be friendly to strangers, give clothes to those who need clothes, care for the sick and show care to those who are in prison. Read verse 40 aloud.

- **When we care for others, whom does Jesus say we are doing it for?**

If we care for others, Jesus says we are caring for Him too. Just as God cares for us and doesn't expect anything in return, we can care for others and not expect anything in return.

Talking to God

One of the best things we can do to care for people in need is to pray for them. Perhaps you know someone who is in need. Maybe someone you know doesn't have enough money to buy food or clothes, is lonely or is sick. Let's pray for others right now and ask God to help us care for those in need. Lead children in prayer, inviting children to tell specific prayer requests.

Getting Crafty
Caring Headband

What Each Child Needs

8-inch (20.5-cm) square of pink or light-
  colored craft foam

pencil

permanent marker

scissors

6x12-inch (15x30.5-cm) piece of craft
  foam (any color)

stapler

craft glue

various craft foam cutouts or sequins

What Each Child Does

1. Using a pencil, draw a large heart shape on the pink or light-colored craft foam. Write "I have a caring heart!" on the heart with a permanent marker. Cut out the heart shape.

2. Cut the other piece of craft foam in half lengthwise. Lay the pieces end to end and have an adult help you staple them together in the middle to form one long band. Glue the heart in place in the center of the band covering the staples.

3. Glue pieces of craft foam or sequins to the headband to decorate it as much as you like.

4. With an adult's help, when the headband has had time to dry, measure it around your head and staple the ends together.

Getting Active

What You Need

masking tape

paper plates

markers

What You Do

1. Divide the playing area in half with a masking tape line.

2. Give each child a paper plate and a marker. Ask children, "What are some things that people need?" (Food, water, friends, family, etc.) Each child writes something that people need on his or her plate. Divide group into two groups. Groups stand on opposite sides of the room. At your signal, all children toss paper plates Frisbee-style across the room.

3. Each child catches or picks up one plate. Child writes an example of a way to care for someone with the need on the plate he or she caught.

4. Children toss and catch plates again. Several children read the needs and responses on plates. Lead children to discuss words and actions that can be used to show care for others the way God cares for us.

Faith Builders at Home

Parents: Use these ideas to help build your child's faith, encouraging your child to become a lifelong follower of Jesus Christ.

"I tell you the truth, whatever you did for one of the least of these brothers of mine, you did for me." Matthew 25:40

Key Word

Care: To express genuine interest or concern.

Quick Pick

At the end of each day for a week, write on a calendar one way a family member cared for someone else. Buy heart stickers and place a sticker on the calendar day each time a family member cares for someone else.

Fun at Home

Use your digital or video camera to photograph family members caring for someone (sharing a snack, doing a chore, etc.).

Steppin' Out

Collect different items to give away (clothes, games, books, etc.). Give the items to an organization that accepts donations to needy people.

Hanging Out in God's House

Lesson 9
Got Church?

"Let us not give up meeting together, as some are in the habit of doing, but let us encourage one another." Hebrews 10:25

Key Word

Encourage: To give help and support.

Opening Up

Who are your friends at church? What do you like to do together? What is your favorite thing about going to church? Invite children to tell ideas.

Checking Out God's Word

It's fun to go to church and spend time with our friends who want to love and obey God. The Bible tells us about something important we can do when we are together at church. Have a child read Hebrews 10:25 aloud.

■ Why do you think some people might stop going to church? Why do you think this verse tells us that we should not give up meeting together?

■ What do you think it means to encourage one another?

When we are at church, we can encourage each other to praise, worship and learn about God. We can help each other love and obey God.

■ What are some of the ways we praise and worship God at church?

■ What are some ways that we learn about loving and obeying God?

Talking to God

Let's encourage each other today by praying for each other. Invite children to tell prayer requests. Lead children in prayer.

Getting Crafty

God's House Magnet

What Each Child Needs

6 craft sticks

2 half-size craft sticks

craft glue

small beads (any color and shape)

$1/2$ piece of card stock (any color)

marker

scissors

magnet

What Each Child Does

1. Glue four craft sticks in the shape of a square. Then glue two craft sticks to form a steeple on the top of the square.

2. Next, use the two small craft sticks to make a cross and glue the cross to the top of the steeple.

3. Glue small beads onto the craft sticks as desired. You can use a few beads or lots of beads, depending on how colorful and decorated you want the church to be.

4. After the glue has had a few minutes to dry, trace around the church onto a piece of card stock. Cut out the shape on the card stock paper and glue it to the back of the church. On the front side, write "Let us not give up meeting together . . ." from Hebrews 10:25.

5. Glue a magnet to the back of the church. Take home the magnet and stick it on your refrigerator.

Getting Active

What You Need

paper

pencils

stopwatch or clock with a second hand

What You Do

1. Give each child a sheet of paper and a pencil. Each child writes one special thing about himself or herself. For example, "I like to ride my bike." Set the timer or stopwatch for one minute.

2. Children have one minute to walk around the room and find other children who enjoy doing the same thing written on the paper. (If you have a larger group, you may want to set the timer for a longer amount of time.) Children sign names on papers. After signing each other's papers, children give each other a high-five to show they've signed each other's papers.

3. When time is up, children count the number of names on his or her paper. Child with the most names tells one thing he or she likes to do at church with his or her friends.

Faith Builders at Home

Parents: Use these ideas to help build your child's faith, encouraging your child to become a lifelong follower of Jesus Christ.

"Let us not give up meeting together, as some are in the habit of doing, but let us encourage one another." Hebrews 10:25

Key Word

Encourage: To give help and support.

Steppin' Out

Choose a day this week to invite a family from your church to meet you at the park for a picnic or at a pizza restaurant. (Optional: Make invitations for the picnic or pizza restaurant day.)

Quick Pick

With your family, read the story in Luke 2:41-52 of Jesus' visit to the Temple in Jerusalem. Talk about your answers to these questions: What was Jesus doing in the Temple? Why do you think Jesus stayed at the Temple? What do you like to do when you go to church?

Fun at Home

Bring your camera to church and take a picture of your child with several friends. Put the picture up on your refrigerator as a reminder to pray for and encourage each other.

Hanging Out in God's House

Lesson 10
All Part of the Body

> "Now you are the body of Christ, and each one of you is a part of it."
> 1 Corinthians 12:27

Key Word

Body of Christ: Members of God's family.

Opening Up

What is something that you are really good at? Invite children to respond.

Checking Out God's Word

Everyone is good at something. But we are probably not all good at the same things. That is because God made each of us with different likes, dislikes, talents and abilities. Let's find out why God created us differently. Have a child read 1 Corinthians 12:14-20.

■ **What do these verses tell us about God?**

■ **What do these verses tell us about ourselves?**

God planned for every person to be different. When we accept Jesus as God's Son, we become members of God's family. In the Bible, God's family is sometimes called "the body of Christ." Read 1 Corinthians 12:27 aloud.

■ **What do you think it means to be a part of the body of Christ?**

As parts of the body of Christ, we all have different jobs to do. There are some people who use their voice to sing for God, some who use their bodies to dance for God, some who teach children about God and so on. Every person's talents are needed to do God's work, just like we need all of the parts of our bodies.

■ **If you were missing part of your body like an eye or an ear, how would your life be different? What if your whole body was just an eye or an ear? How would your life be different?**

■ **What might happen to the body of Christ if you weren't a part of it or you didn't use your abilities the way God wants you to?**

Talking to God

Let's thank God for letting us become members of His family. Let's ask God to help us use the abilities He has given us to do our part in His family. Lead children in prayer.

Getting Crafty
Body of Christ Puzzle

What Each Child Needs

crayons or markers

5x7-inch (12.5x18-cm) piece of paper

glue

5x7-inch (12.5x18-cm) piece of
   craft foam or cardboard

scissors

plastic sandwich bag

What Each Child Does

1. Draw a picture of yourself on the piece of paper. Make it very colorful and fill up as much of the page as you can.

2. Spread a thin layer of glue all over the foam or cardboard. Make sure that it is completely covered.

3. Place the picture you drew on the foam or cardboard and press it down firmly.

4. After the glue is dry, cut the picture into puzzle-shaped pieces.

5. Keep all your pieces in a plastic sandwich bag so you don't lose them.

Getting Active

What You Need

balloons

What You Do

1. **The Bible tells us that when we become members of God's family, we become part of the body of Christ. We can use our abilities and work together in the body of Christ. Let's play a game where we work together.**

2. Divide children into teams of five. Teams line up on one side of the room. Give each child in each line an inflated balloon.

3. At your signal, the first child in each line taps the balloon up into the air as he or she moves to the other side of the playing area and back. The second child in line then taps the balloon across the playing area and back while holding the wrist of the first child. Game continues until the whole team is holding wrists and moving across the playing area and back as the last child taps the balloon. As teams complete the relay, they sit down.

Faith Builders at Home

Parents: Use these ideas to help build your child's faith, encouraging your child to become a lifelong follower of Jesus Christ.

"Now you are the body of Christ, and each one of you is a part of it."
1 Corinthians 12:27

Key Word

Body of Christ: Members of God's family.

Quick Pick

Work on a puzzle as a family. As you put the puzzle together, talk about what the puzzle would be like if a piece was missing. Say 1 Corinthians 12:27 together, with each person saying one word of the verse.

Fun at Home

Cut several slips of paper. Give each family member a pencil. Have each family member write the name of a body part (eyes, ears, legs, feet, etc.) on a slip of paper. Fold papers and place into an empty cup. Shake the cup. Each person picks a slip of paper. Family members take turns reading what is on the paper and telling one way we use that part of the body and why it is important to our bodies. Then see how many abilities you can each name that are important in the body of Christ.

Steppin' Out

Send a thank-you note to someone in your church family who uses his or her abilities to help others in the body of Christ.

Hanging Out in God's House

Lesson 11
God's Piggy Bank

"Each man should give what he has decided in his heart to give, not reluctantly or under compulsion, for God loves a cheerful giver." 2 Corinthians 9:7

Key Word

Tithe: To give God one-tenth of the money you get.

Opening Up

Where do you get money? Do you have an allowance or do you get birthday money? When you receive money, do you save it or spend it? Invite children to respond.

Checking Out God's Word

When we receive money either as a gift or because we've earned it, we can choose what we want to do with the money. The Bible uses the word "tithe" to talk about something important we can do with our money when we come to church. To tithe is to give God one-tenth of what we have. For example, if you had 10 dimes, you could tithe by giving one dime to God.

■ Why do you think God wants us to give Him some of our money?

While God doesn't need our money to do anything, giving a tithe reminds us that God is the one who helps us have ALL the good things in our lives. When we come to church and give to God, it shows how much we love and thank Him.

The Bible also tells us something important about how we should give to God. Have a child read 2 Corinthians 9:7 aloud.

■ What are some ways to show that we are cheerfully giving to God?

■ What are some of the ways our church uses the money we give to God?

Talking to God

Think about what you usually do with the money you get from an allowance or for another reason. It's wise to remember to save some, spend some and give some to God. Let's thank God for all the good things He helps us have, and ask Him to help us learn to give our tithes cheerfully to Him. Lead children in prayer.

Getting Crafty
Money Banks

What Each Child Needs

two cardboard canisters with lids (oatmeal
   or chip containers work well)
paintbrush
glue
decoupage glue or regular white glue that
   has been watered down
small squares of tissue paper (variety of
   colors and patterns)
sharp knife
two small slips of white paper
marker

What Each Child Does

1. Take off the lid of one canister and set it aside.

2. Use a paintbrush to spread some glue over a small part of the surface of the canister. Place a square of tissue paper on the glue and flatten it. Paint over the tissue paper with a small amount of glue.

3. Repeat step 2, overlapping the edges of each new piece of tissue paper, until the entire surface of the canister is covered. Set it aside to begin to dry.

4. Have an adult use the sharp knife to cut a slit in the lid of the canister.

5. Repeat Steps 1 to 4 with the second canister.

6. When both banks are done, use small slips of white paper and a marker to make two labels. One should read "Tithe" and the other should read "Savings." Glue one slip of paper to the front of each canister.

Getting Active

What You Need

bowls

alphabet-shaped cereal

What You Do

1. Pour a large amount of cereal into two bowls. Place bowls on the far side of the playing area.

2. Divide group into two teams. Children line up in the playing area, across from the bowls of cereal letters.

3. At your signal, the first child on each team moves quickly to his or her team's bowl of cereal letters and digs through it to find a T. Child returns to team with letter. The next child moves to the bowl and searches for an I. Relay continues in this manner with each child finding the next letter of the word "tithe." Teams try to form the word "tithe" as many times as possible. Play as time permits.

4. Children from the team who formed the word "tithe" the most times wins.

Faith Builders at Home

Parents: Use these ideas to help build your child's faith, encouraging your child to become a lifelong follower of Jesus Christ.

"Each man should give what he has decided in his heart to give, not reluctantly or under compulsion, for God loves a cheerful giver." 2 Corinthians 9:7

Key Word

Tithe: To give God one-tenth of the money you get.

Fun at Home

Take time to explain to your child how money is given at your church (tithe envelope, collection plate or bucket, etc.). Designate a day when your child can fill out the tithe envelope or place money in the offering bucket or collection plate at church.

Quick Pick

Help your child know what and why you give to God. Your offering of a check once or twice a month, hours of volunteer labor, or use of musical talents, for example, needs to be coupled with a brief explanation. You might say, "Helping to paint the worship building is a way I give to God." Or, "I'm glad to give this money because I'm so thankful for God's love to me."

Steppin' Out

Help your child gain an appreciation for the good things God helps them have by planning a way for your child to become aware of the extreme poverty in which millions of children in our world live. Show current newspaper and/or magazine pictures of others in third-world countries (or even your own country or community). Build on this awareness by determining a way for your family to act in a caring way to help meet the needs of others.

Hanging Out in God's House

Lesson 12
God's Book

"I have hidden your word in my heart that I might not sin against you."
Psalm 119:11

Key Word

Bible: God's book that instructs us how to live.

Opening Up

What is your favorite book to read? Why do you like the book so much? Invite children to tell ideas.

Checking Out God's Word

We all like different books but the Bible is important for all of us to read. Instead of being just one book, the Bible is a collection of many smaller books divided into two main parts—the New Testament and the Old Testament. The Bible tells us what God wants us to know about Himself and His plan for us. This exciting, true story is God's story. That's why another name for the Bible is "God's Word." Psalm 119:11 gives us one reason why it is good to read the Bible. Have a child read Psalm 119:11 aloud. (Optional: Choose the child closest to age 11 to read aloud.)

■ **What does the author of this verse say he's done with God's Word?**

■ **What reason does this verse give for doing that?**

This author tells us that he has hidden God's Word in his heart. That means the author has memorized God's Word. If we memorize God's Word, we can think about it every chance we need to. When we know God's Word, instead of doing wrong things we can remember the right things God says to do in His Word.

■ **Why do you think we are less likely to do wrong things when we know God's Word?**

Talking to God

God's Word is so wonderful. Let's thank God for giving us His Word. Lead children in prayer, allowing children to pray silently. **God, thank You for Your Word. Your Word helps us learn more about You. Help us to obey Your Word every day. In Jesus' name, amen.**

Getting Crafty
Personal Size White Boards

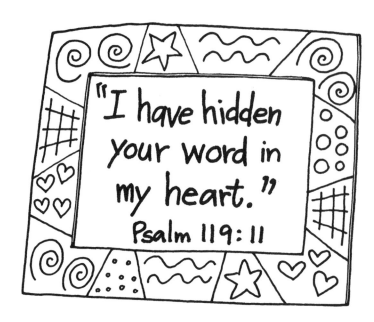

What Each Child Needs

5x7-inch (12.5x18-cm) wooden picture frame with plastic instead of glass (available
   at craft stores)

decorating items (stickers, markers, glitter glue, etc.)

sheet of white paper

scissors

thin-tip dry erase marker

What Each Child Does

1. Disassemble the picture frame, setting aside the back and clear plastic.

2. Decorate wooden frame with markers, glitter glue, stickers, etc.

3. Cut a piece of white paper 5x7-inches (12.5x18-cm) to fit into the frame. As you
   reassemble the frame, make sure that the white paper is visible through the clear
   plastic.

4. Use the dry erase marker to write a Bible verse you want to remember on the
   plastic surface. It will wipe away with a napkin!

Getting Active

What You Need

Bible

ball

What You Do

1. Make copies of the contents page in a Bible. Distribute to children to review.

2. Children stand in a circle. Toss a ball to a child and say "Genesis." Child who catches the ball says "Exodus" and tosses the ball to another child. Continue tossing the ball and saying the names of the books of the Bible in order until all the books have been named. (Optional: For younger children, shorten the number of books to be named.) Repeat game as time permits to see how fast books can be named.

Faith Builders at Home

Parents: Use these ideas to help build your child's faith, encouraging your child to become a lifelong follower of Jesus Christ.

"I have hidden your word in my heart that I might not sin against you."
Psalm 119:11

Key Word

Bible: God's book that instructs us how to live.

Steppin' Out

To put Psalm 119:11 into action, memorize a Bible command together. Try Romans 12:17 or Philippians 4:6-7.

Quick Pick

Ask each family member to answer this question, "What is your favorite Bible story or character? Why?"

Fun at Home

Play a game like Hangman. On a large sheet of paper, draw blank lines for each letter of a Bible book. Family members guess letters of the alphabet. Print correct letters on the appropriate blank lines. Print an incorrect letter to the side of the blank lines and print one letter of the word "Bible." Family members try to guess and find out the correct book in their Bibles before the word "Bible" is completed. Person who guesses the Bible book correctly secretly chooses a different book of the Bible and draws lines for others to guess.

Celebrating Easter

Lesson 13
Welcoming Jesus

"Rejoice in the Lord always. I will say it again: Rejoice!"
Philippians 4:4

Key Word

Welcome: To greet someone with excitement.

Opening Up

Think about what it is like to have a visitor at your house. What kinds of things would you do to get ready for a visitor? Why would you do those things? What would you do if you knew that Jesus was coming to your house? Invite children to tell ideas.

Checking Out God's Word

Today we're going to look at a story in the Bible where a large crowd welcomed Jesus. Read Matthew 21:1-11 aloud. (Optional: Children take turns reading verses aloud.)

- **In verse 8, how did the large crowd welcome Jesus? Why do you think the people did these things?**

- **What do you think a large crowd today might do to welcome Jesus to their city?**

The people in the crowd knew who Jesus was. They welcomed Him by placing their coats on the road where Jesus was traveling and by cutting branches from the trees to place on the road. The crowd honored Jesus by welcoming Him this way.

When we welcome someone, it means to greet him or her with excitement. That's what the people in the large crowd did when they welcomed Jesus. We can welcome Jesus into our lives, too. When we welcome Jesus, it means we believe He is God's Son and our Savior. We show that we are glad for Jesus. Ask a child to read Philippians 4:4 aloud.

Talking to God

Let's pray to Jesus and thank Him for being God's Son and our Savior. Lead children in prayer. **Dear Jesus, You are so great! Thank You for loving us and forgiving our sins. In Your name, amen. If you would like to know more about Jesus' love for you and becoming a member of God's family, please talk to me.** Be available to talk with interested children about salvation. Follow the guidelines in "Leading a Child to Christ" (see p. 10).

Getting Crafty
Welcome Banner

What Each Child Needs

9x12-inch (23x30.5-cm) piece of felt

self-adhesive felt (various colors)

scissors

12-inch (30.5-cm) wooden dowel

fabric glue

clothespins

ribbon

optional—2 dowel caps, paint
  and paintbrushes

What Each Child Does

1. Cut out letters from the self-adhesive felt to spell the word "Welcome." Cut out decorative shapes from self-adhesive felt. Paste letters and decorative shapes onto 9x12-inch piece of felt vertically, making sure to leave 2 inches (5 cm) at the top to wrap around the dowel. (Optional: Use regular felt and fabric glue.) (Optional: Cut out letters to spell small phrases like "Jesus Is Lord.")

2. Wrap the top of the banner around the dowel and glue it into place. Secure it with clothespins until it is dry.

3. While drying, you can cut a desired length of ribbon and tie it securely to each end of the dowel. (Optional: For a more finished look, use dowel caps that can fit on the dowel size you have chosen. You can also paint your dowel and caps to add color.)

Getting Active

What You Need

masking tape

sheets of newspaper

What You Do

1. **To welcome very important people, red carpets are often laid down for people to walk on. Let's make carpets from newspapers and welcome each other.** Use masking tape to make a starting line on one side of the playing area.

2. Divide group into teams of six to eight. Teams line up behind masking tape line. Children on each team form pairs. Give each pair two sheets of newspaper. (Partner with a child if needed.)

3. To move, child's partner places newspaper sheets on floor for child to walk on. First child in each line moves across the room and back, stepping only on sheets of newspaper. Each pair completes the relay twice with a different child moving the newspaper sheets a second time.

4. Repeat relay as time permits, forming new teams and new pairs.

Faith Builders at Home

Parents: Use these ideas to help build your child's faith, encouraging your child to become a lifelong follower of Jesus Christ.

"Rejoice in the Lord always. I will say it again: Rejoice!" Philippians 4:4

Key Word

Welcome: To greet someone with excitement.

Quick Pick

Listen together or sing along to a praise music CD in the car or before bedtime that will help you smile and show joy that Jesus is God's Son and that He's alive today!

Fun at Home

Go to the Internet to research how different cultures welcome one another. For example, in Hawaiian culture, a lei is given to welcome someone with affection. Choose one way that you'd like to do with your family. One day this week, have everyone in your family welcome each other this way.

Steppin' Out

Start a new Easter tradition in your family. Instead of, or in addition to, buying new clothes for yourselves, buy clothes, socks or underwear for a needy family. Give clothing to a community organization to distribute.

Celebrating Easter

Lesson 14
Cleaning Up for Dinner

"Serve one another in love." Galatians 5:13

Key Word

Serve: To do something for others, without expecting anything in return.

Opening Up

What is the dirtiest job you've ever done? Why did you do it? Would you do the job again? Invite children to tell ideas.

Checking Out God's Word

There's a story in the Bible of when Jesus did a "dirty job." Let's read and find out what Jesus did and why He chose to do it. Read John 13:1-17 aloud.

■ **What did Jesus do? Why do you think this job was considered a "dirty job?"**

■ **Why do you think Simon Peter did not want Jesus to wash his feet?**

In Bible times, washing someone's feet was considered a dirty job. People wore torn sandals that left their feet dry and cracked. Some people wore no shoes at all! But that did not matter to Jesus.

Jesus washed the feet of His disciples. This showed that Jesus was willing to serve His disciples. Ask a child to read Galatians 5:13 aloud. **Serving someone**

means that we do things for someone, even if they don't deserve it, without expecting anything in return.

■ **What did Jesus tell His disciples to do for one another?**

■ **How can we follow Jesus' example in our lives today?**

Talking to God

Give everyone a small slip of paper and a pencil. Have each child write his or her name and one way to serve someone (family, friends, neighbors, teachers, pastors, etc.) this week. (Optional: Invite children to tell ideas. List ideas on a large sheet of paper for children to refer to.) Collect the papers and put them in a container. Have each child choose a slip of paper and pair up with the person whose name is on the paper. **With your partners, read each other's slip of paper and pray for one another. Thank God for showing us how to serve one another. Ask God to help your partner serve someone else this week.**

Getting Crafty
Surprise Soap

What Each Child Needs

1 bar of glycerin soap

dull knife

microwave–safe container

microwave

small plastic toys (car, ring, etc.)

Styrofoam cup or paper cup

optional—soap molds in various shapes
  (available at craft stores)

What Each Child Does

1. With an adult's help, unwrap the glycerin soap and cut it up into several pieces for easier melting. Place the pieces in a microwave–safe container and microwave on high power for 30 second increments until melted. Make sure you check after each 30 seconds because it melts fast.

2. Place a small plastic toy in the bottom of a Styrofoam or paper cup. (Optional: For different shapes, use soap molds.)

3. Pour melted soap over the object, completely covering the object.

4. Allow the soap to cool completely, about an hour. (Put it in the refrigerator for quicker results.) When it is cool, tear off the cup.

5. As you use the soap with daily washings, the object will slowly "hatch" out of the soap!

Getting Active

What You Need

two large sheets of butcher paper

crayons

What You Do

1. **One of the ways Jesus showed love to His disciples and served them was by washing their feet during the last meal He ate with them. Let's play a game where we serve each other, too.** Place sheets of paper and crayons on the floor in an open area of the room.

2. All children take off their shoes and place them in a large pile on one side of the playing area. Group children into two equal teams. (If you have more than 14 to 16 children, form more than two teams and limit each team to eight children. If a team has an uneven number of children, play the relay with them.) Assign each team a paper on the floor.

3. Children on each team line up in pairs. At your signal, the first pair in each line runs to his or her team's paper. Children trace each other's feet on the paper and return to their team. Continue until all children have had their feet traced.

4. When tracing is completed, pairs take turns running to the shoe pile. Children must find partner's shoes (with help from partner as needed) and put shoes on partner's feet. Game continues until all children have had their feet traced and are wearing their shoes.

Faith Builders at Home

Parents: Use these ideas to help build your child's faith, encouraging your child to become a lifelong follower of Jesus Christ.

"Serve one another in love." Galatians 5:13

Key Word

Serve: To do something for others, without expecting anything in return.

Steppin' Out

Arrange a family day of service. Choose one day for your family to serve at church, at a community function or at school. Assist with a specific ministry, make and serve food for the homeless in your community or conduct a playground cleanup at your child's school.

Quick Pick

With your family, see how many synonyms for the word "serve" you can think of. After making a list, each person picks his or her favorite synonym and repeats Galatians 5:13 using the synonym.

Fun at Home

Have a foot washing ceremony. Each family member chooses another family member whose feet they will wash at the ceremony.

Celebrating Easter

Lesson 15
It's Not Fair!

"The Lord is full of compassion and mercy." James 5:11

Key Word

Mercy: To forgive someone for a wrong action and show him or her love and kindness that they don't deserve.

Opening Up

Have you ever done something that was wrong? Did you receive a punishment for what you did? What kind of punishment did you receive? Do you think your punishment was fair or unfair? Why? Invite children to respond.

Checking Out God's Word

Everyone has done things that are wrong. It's important to know that when we do wrong things, we can ask God for His forgiveness. When God forgives us, He is showing mercy towards us. When we have mercy for others, we show love and kindness for them, even if they are guilty of doing wrong things. Instead of suffering a punishment for what they've done, they receive forgiveness.

■ In what ways has someone shown you mercy?

The Bible tells us that God's Son, Jesus, took the punishment for our sins when He died on the cross. Read Mark 15.

(Optional: Divide group into pairs or trios to read Mark 15.)

■ Why do you think Jesus was treated so unfairly?

■ Why do you think Jesus took our place and chose to go through so much pain when He didn't have to?

Jesus showed mercy to all of us by dying on the cross. Have a child read James 5:11 aloud. He took the blame for the wrong things people had done, even though He had done nothing wrong. In the Gospel of Luke, the Bible tells us that Jesus even prayed for the people who were hurting Him! He showed mercy to them, too.

Talking to God

Let's say prayers of thanks to Jesus for the mercy He showed us. Invite children to thank Jesus in prayer. End the prayer time by thanking Jesus for His love and asking His help in showing love and mercy to others when they don't deserve it.

Getting Crafty
Cross Plaque

What Each Child Needs

handful of small pebbles

$^3/_4$ cup (180 ml) of plaster of paris

$^1/_4$ cup (60 ml) of water

plastic or paper cup

plastic spoon

small plastic plate

optional—leaves, twigs, dried
flowers, nuts or seashells,
sharp pencil or scissors,
ribbon

What Each Child Does

1. Wash and dry the pebbles. Set them aside.

2. Mix plaster of paris and water in a plastic cup with a plastic spoon for easy clean up. The consistency should be slightly runny, but not watery. Add more plaster of paris or water as needed.

3. With an adult's help, pour the plaster mixture onto the plastic plate. Place the pebbles in the plaster in the shape of a cross. (Optional: Use leaves, twigs, dried flowers, nuts or seashells to create a more detailed picture.)

4. Let the plaster dry completely. Depending on the consistency of the plaster, drying time is about 30 minutes. When it is completely dry, carefully remove it from the plate. (Optional: When the plaster is almost dry, use a sharp pencil or scissors to create a hole at the top of the plaque. String a ribbon through the hole and hang it on the wall.)

Getting Active

What You Need

index card for each child

marker

What You Do

1. **God forgives us for the wrong things we've done, even when we don't deserve it. We're going to play a game that reminds us of God's forgiveness.** On one card print the word "forgiven." Hide all cards around the room.

2. At your signal, each child finds one of the hidden cards. Children with blank cards must do 10 jumping jacks. Child with the word "forgiven" on his or her card does not have to do jumping jacks.

3. Repeat game as time permits, each time choosing a different action (do 10 sit-ups, hop across the room, touch toes, pat head and rub tummy for 10 seconds, etc.) for children with blank cards to perform.

Faith Builders at Home

Parents: Use these ideas to help build your child's faith, encouraging your child to become a lifelong follower of Jesus Christ.

"The Lord is full of compassion and mercy." James 5:11

Key Word

Mercy: To forgive someone for a wrong action and show him or her love and kindness that they don't deserve.

Quick Pick

Ask each person to tell his or her favorite way to celebrate Easter. Just for fun, call a relative like grandma or grandpa and ask him or her, too!

Steppin' Out

Buy a small potted flowering plant. Make and decorate a card that tells about Jesus' love and mercy. Give the card and plant to someone who would be encouraged by a reminder of Jesus' compassion.

Fun at Home

Blow up a balloon. Tap the balloon back and forth repeating one word of James 5:11 each time the balloon is hit. Whenever the balloon touches the ground, repeat the entire verse together.

Celebrating Easter

Lesson 16
The Power of God

"Great is our Lord and mighty in power."
Psalm 147:5

Key Word

Power: To be able to do something.

Opening Up

What are some things that have a lot of power? What are some things that don't have very much power? Invite children to tell ideas.

Checking Out God's Word

A lot of times when we talk about power, we think of things like rocket ships or big machines. The Bible tells us about power, too. One of the most powerful stories in the Bible is found in Matthew 28:1-10. Read Matthew 28:1-10 aloud.

■ How did God show His power in these verses? What did He have power over?

■ If you were alive at that time, and you knew Jesus had died, what would you think if He suddenly appeared in front of you? What would you do?

God raised Jesus from the dead! Not even death could stop God's great power. Have a child read Psalm 147:5 aloud. Because of God's power, Jesus is alive!

■ What did the women do in verse 9 when they saw that Jesus is alive?

■ What are some things we do to worship God for His power over death at Eastertime?

Talking to God

Collect stones for each child. Give each child a permanent marker or help children share markers. Let's use a stone as a reminder of God's power. On your stones, write "Thank You for Your power" or "God Is Power!" Then thank God for His power. Lead children in prayer. Put your stone in a place where it will remind you to thank God for His power during this Eastertime.

Getting Crafty
Jesus Lives Pin

What Each Child Needs

3-inch (7.5-cm) square of brown craft foam

scissors

1-inch (2.5-cm) square of white craft foam

craft glue

fine-point permanent marker

2-inch (5-cm) square of red craft foam

pin back

1-inch (2.5-cm) brown or tan pom-pom

What Each Child Does

1. Cut a small cave shape out of the brown craft foam. Cut a smaller cave shape from the white craft foam.

2. Glue the white craft foam in the middle of the brown craft foam. On the white craft foam write, "Jesus Lives!"

3. Cut out a small cross from the red craft foam (or any color). Glue the red craft foam cross to the top of the brown craft foam cave.

4. Glue a brown pom-pom near the piece of white craft foam to serve as the stone, and glue a pin back to the back of the project just below the cross. (Optional: Make more than one pin and give it to a friend or family member to wear at Eastertime.)

Getting Active

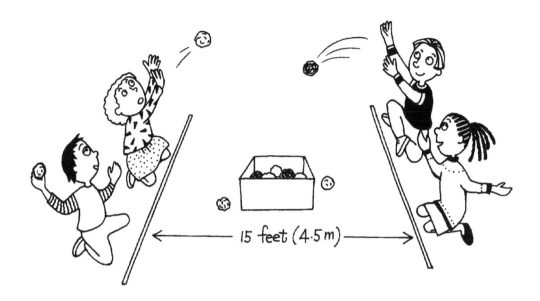

15 feet (4.5 m)

What You Need

masking tape

cardboard box

two colors of scrap paper

watch with second hand or stopwatch

What You Do

1. Make two masking-tape lines 15 feet (4.5 m) apart. Place a cardboard box in the center area.

2. Divide group into two equal teams. Teams sit behind opposite masking-tape lines. Give each team one color of paper (at least 10 sheets for each child on the team). At your signal, children begin making paper balls and throwing them into the box. Call time after 30 seconds.

3. One child from each team collects their team's paper balls from the box and counts them. Another child from each team collects the paper balls landed outside the box and returns them to his or her team. Child from team with the most paper balls in the box tells one way in which God shows His power by helping us in everyday situations.

Faith Builders at Home

Parents: Use these ideas to help build your child's faith, encouraging your child to become a lifelong follower of Jesus Christ.

"Great is our Lord and mighty in power."
Psalm 147:5

Key Word

Power: To be able to do something.

Quick Pick

The Bible is filled with stories about God's power. Choose one story from the Bible that shows God's power and read it with your family this week. (Story Ideas: Exodus 16:1-18; 1 Kings 18:16-39; Mark 4:35-41.)

Fun at Home

Collect several plastic Easter eggs. Each person writes on a slip of paper an Easter message (Jesus is alive! or Jesus lives!, etc.) and places it in an egg. Put all the eggs in a basket. At a mealtime or bedtime, take turns opening the eggs and reading the messages aloud.

Steppin' Out

On your front lawn or at a local park, have a picnic. While you are eating, ask each family member to look around at everything that surrounds them. Ask, "In what ways do you see God's power?" After each family member responds, say a prayer to thank God for His power all around you.

Family Time

Lesson 17
One Big Family

> "You are no longer foreigners and aliens, but fellow citizens with God's people and members of God's household." Ephesians 2:19

Key Word

God's family: People who have accepted God's love through Jesus and who have promised to love God and each other.

Opening Up

How many brothers and sisters do you have? How many aunts, uncles or cousins do you have? Choose a few children to respond. (Optional: Ask all children to hold up the appropriate number of fingers to show answers.)

Checking Out God's Word

Just like we belong to families, God has His own family too! God's family are people who have accepted God's love through Jesus and who have promised to love God and love each other. Let's see what the Bible says about being members of God's family. Have a child read Ephesians 2:19 aloud.

■ **What do you think it means to be an "alien" or "foreigner?"**

■ **What might make an alien or foreigner feel left out?**

■ **When are some times kids your age might feel left out?**

A foreigner in a country might feel left out because he or she doesn't have anything in common with the people who live in that country. But when we choose to accept God's love for us, we're members of God's family. We are not left out! God wants us all to be in His family. He wants us to love and care for the people in His family.

■ **What are some good things about belonging to a family?**

■ **What are some of the benefits of belonging to God's family?**

■ **What are some responsibilities we have to the other people in God's family?**

Talking to God

Let's pray and thank God for making it possible for us to become members of His family. Let's also thank Him for the families that we have. Lead children in prayer. **Dear God, thank You for allowing us to become members of Your family. Show us ways to care for and help each other. Thank You for giving us our families, who love and care for us. In Jesus' name, amen.** Allow an opportunity for children to become members of God's family (see "Leading a Child to Christ" on p. 10).

Getting Crafty
Family Tree

What Each Child Needs

water

brown acrylic paint

plastic cup

paintbrush

11x18-inch (28x45.5-cm) sheet
   of white poster board

newspaper

drinking straw

green construction paper

scissors

markers

glue stick

What Each Child Does

1. With an adult's help, mix equal parts of water and brown paint in plastic cup. Using mixture, paint a tree trunk on the poster board. Hold the poster board upside down over a sheet of newspaper and let paint drip down to form tree branches. Tilt poster board from side-to-side as paint drips to change direction of branches. After branches are formed, create more small branches and twigs by blowing paint on the paper through a drinking straw.

2. Set painting aside to dry. Draw and cut several leaves from green construction paper. Write the names of each of your family members on the leaves. Do not forget to include grandparents, cousins, etc.

3. Your painting should be dry enough to glue leaves on the branches. Use markers to draw additional items such grass, the sun, birds, etc.

4. Hang your picture somewhere in your house where your family will see it on a regular basis. Use the painting as a reminder to pray for each member of your family.

Getting Active

What You Need

volleyball or tennis ball

optional—name tags

What You Do

1. **Shortly before Jesus returned to heaven, He promised to be with the members of His family both now and in the future. Let's play a game where we call out each other's names to remember that we can all be members of God's family.**

2. (Optional: Children wear name tags or review names of classmates before playing game.) Children stand in a circle. Choose one child to stand in the center of the circle and be the Ball Tosser. Ball Tosser throws ball straight up in the air and calls the name of one of the children. Child whose name was called moves to get the ball, becoming the Ball Catcher. All other children move around the playing area, attempting to move away from the Ball Catcher. When the Ball Catcher gets the ball, he or she calls out "Freeze" and all other children must freeze.

3. Ball Catcher rolls the ball at any of the other children who must be standing on one foot but can lean out of the way of the ball. The child who is first touched by the ball becomes the Ball Tosser for the next round. If the ball does not touch any child, the Ball Catcher becomes the new Ball Tosser. Children return to circle position and the new Ball Tosser throws the ball again, calling out the name of a different child. Repeat play as time allows.

Faith Builders at Home

Parents: Use these ideas to help build your child's faith, encouraging your child to become a lifelong follower of Jesus Christ.

"You are no longer foreigners and aliens, but fellow citizens with God's people and members of God's household." Ephesians 2:19

Key Word

God's family: People who have accepted God's love through Jesus and who have promised to love God and each other.

Quick Pick

Look at pictures of your family in a photo album or on a video. (Challenge: How many different relatives can you find pictures of?) Talk about how God's family is made up of many different people just like your family.

Steppin' Out

Think of a family from your church with whom you would like to become better acquainted. Invite the family to join you for pizza or go out for ice cream together.

Fun at Home

Make peanut butter clay. (Optional: Purchase play dough.) Mix equal parts of peanut butter and dry powdered milk. Slowly add honey to reach desired thickness. If mixture is too sticky, add more milk. Mold the clay into small people to represent each member of your family. (Optional: Use pretzels, raisins and sunflower seeds for eyes, hair and nose on your clay people.)

Family Time

Lesson 18
Mother's Day

"Honor your mother and your father."
Ephesians 6:2

Key Word

Respect: To treat someone the way you want to be treated.

Opening Up

If you could design the perfect parents, what would they be like? What would make them such good parents? Invite children to tell ideas.

Checking Out God's Word

God gives us people like moms, dads, grandmas and grandpas to love and care for us. (Note: Be sensitive to the family situations represented in your group. Include references to specific caregivers as needed.) **The Bible tells us how God would like us to treat the people who love and care for us.** Read Ephesians 6:1-3 aloud.

- **What is the command given in these verses?**

- **Why might it be hard for a kid your age to obey these commands? Why might it be easy for a kid your age to obey these commands?**

The command in these verses says to honor your parents. Another word for "honor" is "respect." To show someone respect means to treat him or her the way you would like to be treated. Read Ephesians 6:2-3 aloud again.

- **What promise does God make to those who show respect to their moms and dads?**

- **What are some ways that kids your age can show respect to their parents and others who care for them?**

Talking to God

Think about a time this past week when you showed respect to your mom or dad. Then think about a time when you did not show respect to your mom or dad. What could you have done differently? Allow time for children to think of their responses. **Today we're going to pray and thank God for our parents and ask Him to help us show respect to our parents this week.** Lead children in prayer. Children may fill in the prayer aloud or silently. **Dear God, thank You for giving us parents and other people who love and care for us. Help us to show respect to them by . . . . In Jesus' name, amen.**

Getting Crafty
Decoupage Vase

What Each Child Needs

old magazines

scissors

water

glue

plastic bowl

paint brush

empty water bottle with the top cut off

spray sealer

What Each Child Does

1. Think of an adult to whom you want to give a special gift (mom, dad, teacher, grandma).

2. Search through old magazines and cut out pictures of things that this person likes. Also look for words and phrases that describe the person.

3. Mix one part water with two parts glue in a plastic bowl. Paint a layer of glue over a small section of the water bottle. Place one of the pictures or words on the bottle and smooth out. Paint another layer of glue over the picture to secure in place. Repeat process until the bottle is covered with pictures or words.

4. With an adult's help, after vase is dry, coat with a sealer spray to protect it from water. (Optional: Put flowers in the vase before giving it as a gift.)

Getting Active

What You Need

container (wastebasket, cardboard box)

ball

What You Do

1. Children line up approximately 3 feet (.9 m) from container.

2. Children take turns bouncing a ball at least once while attempting to get ball into container. If the ball goes into the container, child tells the name of someone who guides and cares for him or her. If ball does not go into container after three tries, next child takes a turn. Continue play as time allows.

Faith Builders at Home

Parents: Use these ideas to help build your child's faith, encouraging your child to become a lifelong follower of Jesus Christ.

"Honor your mother and your father."
Ephesians 6:2

Key Word

Respect: To treat someone the way you want to be treated.

Quick Pick

Look around the room and count the number of windows. Then see if you can list that number of ways a mom, grandma or other female relative has shown care for your family. Repeat activity by counting the number of doors, switch plates, etc. (Optional: List ways family members can show respect to each other.)

Fun at Home

Think of familiar commercials. Just for fun, rewrite the commercials so that they encourage people to show respect to others. Write your commercials on large Post-it Notes and put them up around the house or in the car as reminders to treat others with respect.

Steppin' Out

Help your child use a video camera to interview family members, someone at church, school or in your neighborhood. Interviewees complete the sentence, "The best way to show respect to someone is to . . . ."

Family Time

Lesson 19
Jesus Loves the Children

"Let the little children come to me, and do not hinder them, for the kingdom of God belongs to such as these." Mark 10:14

Key Word

Bless: To ask God to do good things for another person.

Opening Up

When are some times it is really fun to be a kid? When are some times it is hard to be a kid? What are some examples of times or places when kids are told to be quiet or sit still? Invite children to respond.

Checking Out God's Word

In the Bible there was a time when Jesus' disciples wanted some children to be quiet and to leave Jesus alone. Let's read and find out what happened. Have a child read Mark 10:13-16 aloud.

■ Why were people bringing their children to Jesus?

■ Why do you think the disciples rebuked or turned away the children? How do you think the children felt when they heard the words of the disciples?

■ What did Jesus say to His disciples when He saw what they were doing? How do you think the children felt then?

Jesus showed how much He loved the children by welcoming them. He took them in His arms and blessed them. The word "bless" means to ask God to do good things for someone else. Jesus loves you just as much as He loved those children in the Bible. We can't see Jesus in person, but we can spend time getting to know Him by reading stories about Him and praying.

Talking to God

Have children close their eyes. **Imagine that you are standing near Jesus. Jesus is glad to see you and He gives you a big hug. Think about how much Jesus loves you. Today we're going to pray and thank Jesus for His love.** Lead children in prayer. **Dear Jesus, thank You for loving each of us. We love You, too. In Your name, amen.**

Getting Crafty

Jesus Loves Me Bookmark

What Each Child Needs

glue stick

$3^1/_2$ x $8^1/_2$-inch (9x21.5-cm) piece of cardstock

3x8-inch (7.5x20.5-cm) piece of cardstock in a second color

$2^1/_2$ x $7^1/_2$-inch (6.5x19-cm) piece of cardstock in a third color

adhesive letter stickers

heart-shaped stickers

other decorative stickers

hole punch

8-inch (20.5-cm) length of ribbon

What Each Child Does

1. Make bookmark by gluing the three pieces of cardstock one on top of the other so that a small portion of the larger pieces are showing around the edges of the smaller pieces.

2. Attach letter stickers to write "Jesus Loves . . . " on the bookmark (inserting your name). Use heart-shaped stickers and other decorative stickers to decorate bookmark.

3. Punch a hole in the top edge of the bookmark and tie a ribbon through it. (Optional: Make additional bookmarks to give as gifts to family, friends, teachers, etc.)

Getting Active

What You Need

masking tape

playground ball or basketball

What You Do

1. **Let's play a game to remind us of the ways Jesus showed His love when He lived on Earth.**

2. Use masking tape to mark a starting line.

3. Select a volunteer to be the bowler. The remaining children—the human bowling pins—stand approximately 10 feet (3 m) away from the starting line in bowling-pin formation (see sketch). Children stand one arm's length apart (when arm is extended, child's fingertips touch a nearby child's shoulders).

4. Bowler names a way Jesus showed love (welcomed the children, made a blind man to see, taught about God, healed a lame man, died on the cross, forgave sins, etc.) and rolls ball, trying to hit the feet of one of the human bowling pins. The "pins" must keep their left feet on the floor, but they may move their right feet to avoid being hit by the ball. First child hit with the ball becomes the bowler for the next round. Continue game as time permits.

Faith Builders at Home

Parents: Use these ideas to help build your child's faith, encouraging your child to become a lifelong follower of Jesus Christ.

> "Let the little children come to me, and do not hinder them, for the kingdom of God belongs to such as these." Mark 10:14

Key Word

Bless: To ask God to do good things for another person.

Quick Pick

As part of a mealtime or bedtime prayer, pray for your child and ask God to bless him or her in a specific way. Invite your child to pray for a family member, too.

Steppin' Out

Visit the nursery at your church or a daycare center in your neighborhood. As a way of following Jesus' example of showing love to children, talk to the director and arrange a time for your family to assist with games and activities with young children.

Fun at Home

Print the words of Mark 10:14 on a large sheet of paper, dividing the verse into seven or eight phrases. Family members sit around the large sheet of paper you prepared. Play a game similar to Hot Potato. As you play music, family members pass a ball or stuffed animal to each other. When music stops, person holding ball or stuffed animal says the first phrase of the verse. Other family members take turns saying the next phrases. Continue until the entire verse has been quoted. Last person places a piece of candy on a word on the paper. Repeat activity until all the words are covered with candy. Enjoy candy together!

Family Time

Lesson 20
Listen Up!

"Listen to advice and accept instruction, and in the end you will be wise."
Proverbs 19:20

Key Word

**Wisdom: To think and act in right ways that show
love and obedience to God.**

Opening Up

(Note: You may wish to complete first portion of craft activity on the next page before this lesson to allow time for paintings to dry.) **Let's play a game called "Mother, May I?"** Choose a child to be "mother." Volunteer stands on one side of the room. All other children stand at the other end of the room. Children stand facing volunteer. Volunteer gives instructions for children to follow, for example, "(Kelly), take five baby steps forward." Child must ask "Mother, May I?" before following instructions. Mother replies, "Yes, you may." If child does not ask for permission or moves before receiving permission, he or she moves back to the starting point. First child to reach and tag "mother" wins.

Checking Out God's Word

Listening to the instructions others like our parents give us isn't always easy. But paying attention to instructions can make a big difference in our lives. Let's see what the Bible says about listening to instructions from others. Have a child read Proverbs 19:20 aloud.

■ **What does this verse say we should do? Why?**

■ **What advice have your parents given you?**

■ **Why might it be hard for kids your age to listen to the advice of their parents?**

■ **What will happen if we listen to advice and accept instruction?**

When we're wise, it means that we can think and act in right ways. God cares for us so much that He has given us people who will give us the kind of advice and instruction we need to become wise as we grow.

Talking to God

Today we'll pray to God and thank Him for the people who guide us and help us become wise. Then we'll ask God for His help to become good listeners. Lead children in prayer. **Dear God, thank You for the people in our lives who guide us and help us so that we can become wise. In Jesus' name, amen.**

Getting Crafty
Scratchy Paintings

What Each Child Needs

crayons

8¹/₂ x 11-inch (21.5x28-cm)
  sheet of cardstock

dish soap

black paint

plastic cup

newspaper

paint brush

toothpick

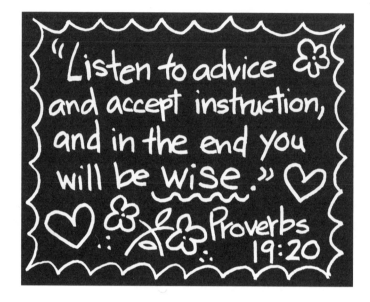

What Each Child Does

1. Color the entire sheet of cardstock. Press down hard while you are coloring. Use lots of colors in any kind of desired pattern.

2. With an adult's help, mix a few drops of dish soap with black paint in a plastic cup. Paint mixture over entire sheet of colored stock paper. Make sure that sheet is completely covered, but not so thick that it won't dry.

3. Set painting aside to dry. (Note: You may wish to complete lesson on previous page while paintings dry.)

4. When painting is dry, use the pointy tip of a toothpick to scratch black paint away and write Proverbs 19:20 on the cardstock. (Optional: Choose one or two key words of the verse to write.) You may also use the toothpick to scratch designs around the edges of the verse.

Getting Active

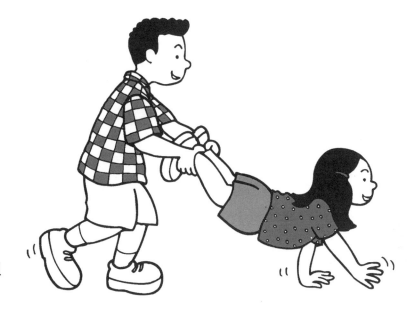

What You Need

Bible

markers

index cards

masking tape

two baskets

clothespins

What You Do

1. Write the words of Proverbs 19:20 on index cards, writing one word on each card. Make two sets of cards. Use masking tape to make a starting line and finish line at least 20 feet (6 m) apart on the floor. Place baskets on finish line.

2. Divide group into two teams. Each team lines up behind starting line. Place one set of cards next to each team. At your signal, the first child on each team clips an index card to his or her clothing and pretends to be the Wheelbarrow steered by the next child in line. The Wheelbarrow walks on hands toward the basket while the partner steers by holding the wheelbarrow's feet (see sketch). At the basket, the Wheelbarrow stands up, drops card into basket, gives the clothespin to the partner and runs to the back of the line. The partner returns to the front of the line and is the next Wheelbarrow. Once everyone has had a turn to be the Wheelbarrow, entire team goes to basket and assembles index cards in verse order. First team to assemble verse in order wins!

Faith Builders at Home

Parents: Use these ideas to help build your child's faith, encouraging your child to become a lifelong follower of Jesus Christ.

> "Listen to advice and accept instruction, and in the end you will be wise."
> Proverbs 19:20
>
> ## Key Word
>
> **Wisdom: To think and act in right ways that show love and obedience to God.**

Steppin' Out

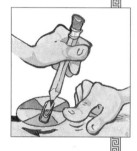

Using a sheet of paper, a pencil and a paper clip, make a spinner as shown in the sketch. Divide the spinner into four sections. Write a place your child goes in each section (school, church, mall, park, etc.). Have your child spin the paper clip and use the word the clip points to in a sentence that tells some good advice or instruction to follow while at the location. Talk about how following the advice or instruction will show love and obedience to God.

Fun at Home

Watch a family TV show together. After the show, write down the choices that the main character(s) made during the show. Talk about the results of the choices, which choices were wise and similar situations your child might face.

Quick Pick

At bedtime, meal time, or while driving in the car, ask your child to tell the most helpful advice or instruction someone gave him or her today (or this week). Then share with your child the best advice you've ever received. Tell your children how the advice helped you make a wise choice.

Family Time

Lesson 21
Friends in the Family

> "How good and pleasant it is when brothers live together in unity!"
> Psalm 133:1

Key Word

Unity: To live in peace with others.

Opening Up

What's something a kid your age might like about having a brother or sister? What's something a kid your age might NOT like about having a brother or sister? Invite children to respond.

Checking Out God's Word

There are always going to be times when we have a hard time getting along with the people in our families. As we talk about getting along with brothers and sisters today, if you don't have a brother or sister, think about how you can get along with your friends, or your parents. Let's see what God's Word says about getting along with others. Have a child read Psalm 133:1 aloud. This verse uses the word "brothers," but it also means brothers and sisters.

- What do you think it means to live in unity with someone?

- What kind of actions show that you are living in unity, or living in peace, with someone else?

- How might brothers and sisters who are living in unity treat each other?

- What words does this verse use to describe what it's like to live in unity with someone?

- What words would describe what it's like when brothers and sisters don't live peacefully together?

Whether you have a brother or sister or not, God knows that it is best when we can live in peace with others. He promises to help us talk and act in ways that show unity. Invite several children to name ways to live in peace with brothers and sisters.

Talking to God

One of the best ways to live in unity with others is to ask God for help. As we pray today, let's first thank God for giving us brothers and sisters. Then, second, we can ask His help in getting along with the people in our families. Lead children in prayer. Dear God, thank You for giving us brothers, sisters, parents and friends. Help us to show Your love to others so that we can live with one another in unity. In Jesus' name, amen.

Getting Crafty
"Some Buggy Loves You" Frame

What Each Child Needs

two 5$\frac{1}{2}$ x 8-inch (14x20.5-cm) pieces of cardstock or poster board

scissors

markers

stamp pads in a variety
  of colors

disposable wipes

glue

What Each Child Does

1. Set one of the pieces of poster board aside to use as the back of the frame. Fold the other piece of poster board in half. With an adult's help, cut a rectangular-shaped hole in the center. This is where the photo will show through.

2. Open the folded poster board. Write "Some Buggy Loves You" at bottom of the frame. Press your thumb on stamp pad and then onto the frame to make thumbprints. Repeat this process around the entire frame. Use a marker to draw antennae and legs to turn each thumbprint into a bug, caterpillar, ladybug or other insect. Draw leaves or grass with markers.

3. Turn the frame over and apply glue to only three sides of the frame. Place it on the other piece of poster board that you set aside earlier.

4. Take home your frame and insert a photo of you and your siblings (or friends or parents) inside it. Give your photo as a gift to a brother or sister, or keep it handy as a reminder to pray for your family.

Getting Active

What You Need

ball of yarn the same size for every four to six children

optional—crepe paper roll

What You Do

1. Children count off to form teams of four to six players. Teams form single-file lines in center of playing area, leaving plenty of space between teams.

2. Give the first child in each line a ball of yarn. (Optional: Use crepe paper roll.) The first child holds the end of the yarn to his or her stomach with one hand and then passes the ball of yarn to the next child in line. Children continue passing yarn to child at the end of the line who wraps it around his or her back and passes it back to the front of the line. (Note: Make sure children do not wrap themselves too tight.) Passing continues until children have wrapped themselves (from the waist down) with the entire ball of yarn. (Note: Children should stand as close together as possible to speed up the wrapping process.) The first team to finish names a way to live with others in unity.

Faith Builders at Home

Parents: Use these ideas to help build your child's faith, encouraging your child to become a lifelong follower of Jesus Christ.

"How good and pleasant it is when brothers live together in unity!"
Psalm 133:1

Key Word

Unity: To live in peace with others.

Fun at Home

Use a marker or crayon to write a number from 0 to 9 on a blank sheet of paper. Make a numbered paper for each person in the family. On the numbered paper, each person draws a picture of something he or she enjoys doing with other family members (playing soccer, reading books, playing video games, hiking, riding bikes, etc.). He or she draws the picture using the number written on the paper. For example, turn the number two into a picture of a soccer ball. Talk about actions that help you live in unity when participating in the activities pictured.

Quick Pick

See if your family can quote Psalm 133:1 while doing jumping jacks, or jogging in place.

Steppin' Out

Choose a day this week to make each family member a V.I.P. Each person thanks the V.I.P. for something helpful he or she has done this week. Then let the V.I.P. choose a favorite food for dinner, dinnertime music to listen to, a favorite game to play and/or a favorite book to read aloud.

Watch Your Words

Lesson 22
When I'm Angry

"Do everything without complaining or arguing, so that you may become blameless and pure." Philippians 2:14-15

Key Word

Argue: To disagree in an angry way.

Opening Up

What do kids your age often argue about? When was the last time you argued with someone? What was the argument about? Invite children to respond.

Checking Out God's Word

We are not always going to agree with everyone about everything. It's normal not to agree with others all the time. The Bible has some good advice for us when we don't agree with someone else. Read Philippians 2:14-15 aloud.

■ What's the main idea of these verses?

■ How should we act, even when we don't agree with others?

■ Why might it be hard for a kid your age not to argue with others?

The Bible says that when we choose not to argue with others we can be blameless and pure. That means we are doing our best to show by our words that we want to love God and show His love to others. The end of verse 15 says that when we don't argue with others it's like we are shining stars in the darkness. Our kind actions help others see what it's like to be followers of God.

■ What are some things we can do when we are tempted to get into an argument? What can we do instead of arguing? (Ask God for help in not arguing. Walk away from the person. Count to 10. Remember to use kind words.)

Talking to God

Think of someone who you might be temped to argue with. Pause briefly. Let's pray and ask God's help in choosing not to argue with others. Lead children in prayer. **Dear God, thank You for being able to help us when we are tempted to argue with others. We want to be examples of Your love. In Jesus' name, amen.**

Getting Crafty
Pasta Magnet

What Each Child Needs

newspaper

lasagna noodle

alphabet pasta

pasta in a variety of shapes

acrylic paint in assorted colors

paintbrushes

craft glue

2 magnets

What Each Child Does

1. Cover work surface with newspaper. Carefully break one lasagna noodle to a desired length, unless you want to use the entire length of the noodle. Paint one side of the noodle. Set noodle aside to dry.

2. Pick out pasta letters to spell "DO EVERYTHING WITHOUT ARGUING." Paint letters a color that will contrast with the color you painted the lasagna noodle. Set pasta letters aside to dry.

3. Choose other pasta shapes to use as decorations and paint shapes as desired. Set aside to dry.

4. Glue the two magnets to the back of the lasagna noodle. Turn lasagna noodle over and glue the painted pasta letters onto lasagna noodle in the correct order. Glue the other noodles where desired. Let everything dry completely.

5. Take home the magnet and hang it on refrigerator to remember not to argue with others.

Getting Active

What You Need

Bibles

index cards in a variety of colors

marker

scissors

What You Do

1. Print the words of Philippians 2:14-15 on index cards, one word on each card. Cut cards in half. Hide the pieces in the room for children to find. Make a set of same-colored cards for each small group of children.

2. Children form as many groups as card sets you made. Invite the groups to search for pieces of the verse cards. Once a child finds the first card, his or her group keeps looking for the same-colored cards.

3. Children place cards together to find the words of the verse. Children find verse in their Bibles and put cards in order. Children read verse together.

Faith Builders at Home

Parents: Use these ideas to help build your child's faith, encouraging your child to become a lifelong follower of Jesus Christ.

"Do everything without complaining or arguing, so that you may be blameless and pure." Philippians 2:14-15

Key Word

Argue: To disagree in an angry way.

Fun at Home

On separate small pieces of paper write these words: God, problem, pray, argue, kind, love, help, me, friend, disagree, act, say. Put the slips of paper, along with several blank pieces of paper, in a bag or container. Each person takes a turn to choose three pieces of paper. Then he or she makes up a sentence which includes the three words (blank papers can represent any word). The sentence should tell something about how God wants us to act when we are tempted to argue with others.

Steppin' Out

Your child will learn more about not arguing from your example than from your words. In the days to come, be on the lookout for ways you can model calmness for your child in a tense situation. In an appropriate situation, explain to your child why you were angry. Then tell what you did instead of arguing. For example, "I was so angry that my car was not fixed yet. But instead of arguing with the mechanic, I decided to go for a walk and talk to the mechanic later when I was calm."

Quick Pick

Read one of these Proverbs about wise actions together and then choose one to memorize as a family: Proverbs 10:12; 12:18; 15:1.

Watch Your Words

Lesson 23
Build Each Other Up

"Therefore encourage one another and build each other up,
just as in fact you are doing." 1 Thessalonians 5:11

Key Word

Build Each Other Up: To encourage and help someone with your words.

Opening Up

Let's play a fun game. Choose a volunteer to balance an object (book, paper plate, marker, etc.) on his or her head for 30 seconds while walking around the room. **While (Evan) tries to balance the (book) on (his) head, I'd like everyone else to cheer for (him) and build (him) up by saying positive comments. For example, "You can do it, (Evan)!"** As time permits, allow other volunteers to take a turn balancing the object.

Checking Out God's Word

When you have something hard to do, it's great to hear the encouragement and cheers of other people.

■ **When are some times kids your age need others to encourage and cheer them on?**

The Bible tells us about encouraging others and cheering for them. Read 1 Thessalonians 5:11 aloud.

■ **What does this verse say we can do for others?**

■ **What are some ways of building up other people?**

■ **Who is someone who has encouraged and helped you by his or her words? What did the person say?**

■ **What are some words kids can say to encourage and build each other up?**

Using our words to encourage and help others is a way of showing God's love to them. We build them up so they can continue to do what God says is right.

Talking to God

Children sit in a circle. **Today we'll encourage each other by thanking God for the person sitting to our right.** Make sure that each child knows the name of the person to his or her right. Begin the prayer by saying, **Thank You, God, for (Kimberly).** (Kimberly) continues the prayer by thanking God for the person sitting to (her) right. Continue until each person has been prayed for. End the prayer time by thanking God for His love and asking His help in encouraging and building up each other.

Getting Crafty
Encouragement Pennants

What Each Child Needs

scissors

8$\frac{1}{2}$ x 11-inch (21.5x28-cm) piece of felt

12-inch (30.5-cm) wooden dowel

stapler

fabric puffy paint

craft glue

pom-poms

What Each Child Does

1. Think of someone you want to encourage and build up.

2. Cut a pennant shape from felt piece. Fold side edge of felt over about 1-inch (2.5-cm) and staple it three or four times, creating a pocket for wooden dowel to slide in.

3. Using the puffy paint, write on the felt a phrase that will encourage the person to whom you are giving the pennant.

4. Glue pom-poms on felt as decorations. Let dry completely.

5. Give your pennant to the person you want to encourage.

Getting Active

What You Need

large sheets of paper

masking tape

Post-it Notes

stopwatch or watch with a second hand

What You Do

1. **We can encourage and build each other up as a way of showing God's love. Let's play a game where we work together to build a wall.**

2. Tape two large sheets of paper on one wall of the room, leaving space between the two papers. Place a large stack of Post-it Notes next to each paper.

3. Group children into two teams. Teams line up on opposite side of the playing area from the sheets of paper.

4. At your signal, start your stopwatch and send the first child on each team to his or her team's paper. Child sticks a Post-it Note onto the bottom part of the paper and then returns to line. Next child in line runs to wall and repeats action. Children on each team continue taking turns building their team's wall. Invite children to cheer for their team members.

5. After several minutes, call time. Compare the walls built and ask a volunteer from the team with the largest wall to tell a situation in which a child needs encouragement. If time allows, turn papers over for children to play again.

Faith Builders at Home

Parents: Use these ideas to help build your child's faith, encouraging your child to become a lifelong follower of Jesus Christ.

> "Therefore encourage one another and build each other up, just as in fact you are doing." 1 Thessalonians 5:11

Key Word

Build Each Other Up: To encourage and help someone with your words.

Steppin' Out

Look on the Internet or in a book from the library to find sign language for the words "encourage" and "build." Practice the signs as you say the words of 1 Thessalonians 5:11 together.

Fun at Home

On a large sheet of paper, draw a stick figure person. Then, as a family, list the many abilities God has given people and the ways they may use them to help others (ears to be a good listener, mouth to pray for others, hands to help with chores, etc.). Write each ability near the appropriate body part. After completing your list, tell your child one or two abilities you think God has given him or her.

Quick Pick

Build each other up by thinking of a nickname for each member of your family that tells a good characteristic about each one (Helpful Hannah, Super-Singer Sami, etc.).

Watch Your Words

Lesson 24
Father's Day

> "The Lord is good to all; he has compassion on all he has made." Psalm 145:9

Key Word

Compassion: To understand someone's feelings and offer kindness to him or her.

Opening Up

What are some things that a good father does? What do you like to do with your dad, grandpa or uncle? Invite children to respond. (Note: Be sensitive to the family situations represented in your group. Include references to specific caregivers as needed.)

Checking Out God's Word

It's fun to think about the things we like to do with our dads and other people who take care of us. The Bible tells a story about a father and son. Listen to find out how they felt about each other. Have a child who enjoys reading to read Luke 15:11-24 aloud to the group.

- **What did the younger son do with the money his father gave him?**

- **How do you think the father felt when his son left?**

- **How do you think the younger son felt when he finally went home to his father? Do you think the son was afraid? Why or why not?**

- Read verse 20 aloud. **What did the father do when his son returned home?**

The father in this story was loving and compassionate. God is like a perfect father to us. He is ready to forgive and show compassion to us, no matter what we've done. Psalm 145:9 says "The Lord is good to all; he has compassion on all he has made." When we have done something wrong and disobeyed God, He looks on us with compassion and welcomes us. We can always tell Him we are sorry, just like the son in this story did.

Talking to God

Think about God's love and compassion for you. If you want to tell Him you are sorry for a wrong action, you can do that right now. Give children a few minutes to pray silently. Then end the prayer time by thanking God for our fathers and for being the best father of all. **Dear God, thank You for the people You give us who care for us. Thank You for the love and compassion You show us, even when we have disobeyed You. We love You. In Jesus' name, amen.**

Getting Crafty
Dad Rocks! Paper Weight

What Each Child Needs

3- to 4-inch (7.5- to 10-cm) rock

acrylic paint in various colors

paintbrushes in various sizes

spray sealer

What Each Child Does

1. Think of someone (dad, grandpa, uncle, teacher, coach) to whom you want to give a special gift.

2. Look at your rock. What object does it remind you of? What do you want to turn your rock into? You might try a football, basketball, bug, dog or dinosaur.

3. Paint your rock however you want to make it look like the object you thought of. Take your time and be creative!

4. On one side of the rock, paint the words "(Dad) Rocks!" Use the name of the person to whom you are giving your gift.

5. Let paint dry completely. With an adult's help, spray with sealer. The sealer will keep your rock from chipping or getting ruined if anything spills on it.

6. Give the gift to the special person you want to honor.

Getting Active

What You Need

index cards

marker

What You Do

1. **In our game today, we'll pretend to be some different kinds of people. Our game will remind us that God has compassion and cares for everyone!** Print each of these kinds of people on separate index cards: baby, old person, basketball player, soccer player, toddler, movie star, teenager, race car driver, juggler.

2. Group children into two equal teams. Teams line up on one side of an open area in your room. Stand between the two teams.

3. At your signal, the first child in each team runs to you. Show him or her one of the cards you prepared. Child returns to his or her team and then moves across the room and back as though he or she is a (basketball player). Children continue taking turns until all children on the team have had a turn. Play as many rounds of the game as time permits.

Faith Builders at Home

Parents: Use these ideas to help build your child's faith, encouraging your child to become a lifelong follower of Jesus Christ.

"The Lord is good to all; he has compassion on all he has made." Psalm 145:9

Key Word

Compassion: To understand someone's feelings and offer kindness to him or her.

Quick Pick

Cover the dining room table with a large sheet of paper or give everyone a sheet or two of scratch paper. Set out a variety of colored markers and let everyone doodle words and pictures that complete the sentence "My favorite thing about (dad, grandpa, favorite uncle, etc.) is the way he. . . ." At the end of the meal, give the paper(s) to the person you wrote or drew about.

Fun at Home

As a family, show compassion for someone who is in need (grandparent died, someone in a car accident, someone who is ill, etc.). Write letters or design cards to mail or personally deliver.

Steppin' Out

Make or buy extra meals at a mealtime with your family. Have your family deliver the meals to a homeless shelter or another shelter that accepts meal donations.

Watch Your Words

Lesson 25
Lying

> "The Lord detests lying lips, but he delights in men who are truthful."
> Proverbs 12:22

Key Word

Lying: Saying something on purpose that is not true.

Opening Up

What's a game you really like? What's a game you don't like at all? Invite volunteers to answer. Repeat questions about several other items such as foods, drinks, smells, etc.

Checking Out God's Word

Today we're going to be talking about something that the Bible says God doesn't like at all. In fact, the Bible says He hates this thing! Let's find out what it is. Have a child read Proverbs 12:22 aloud.

■ **What word does this verse use for the word "hate?"**

■ **Why do you think God hates it when people lie?**

■ **How does God feel about people who tell the truth?**

Even though this verse tells us that God hates our lies, it doesn't say that God hates the people who tell lies. That's good to know because we need God's love and help to tell the truth.

■ **When are some times it's hard for kids your age to tell the truth?**

■ **Why is it important to tell the truth? How would you feel about someone who told you lies?**

Sometimes telling the truth isn't easy, but it's better to tell the truth so that our friends and the people in our families know they can trust us to be honest.

Talking to God

Today we can pray and ask God to forgive us for the times we've lied to others. We can ask for His help in telling the truth, even when it may seem hard. Lead children in prayer, allowing for a brief time of silent prayer. **Dear God, thank You for loving us, even when we've disobeyed You. Thank You for forgiving us. Help us to tell the truth. In Jesus' name, amen.**

Getting Crafty
No Lying Place Mat

What Each Child Needs

pattern scissors

ruler

two 12x18-inch (30.5x45.5-cm) pieces
   of craft foam in two different colors

9x12-inch (23x30.5-cm) piece of red
   craft foam

9x12-inch (23x30.5-cm) piece of black
   craft foam

scissors

craft glue

optional—letter stencils, pencils

What Each Child Does

1. Use pattern scissors to trim $1/2$-inch (1.3-cm) off each side of one of the large
   pieces of craft foam. Glue trimmed piece of craft foam to the top of the other
   large piece of craft foam. This will be the place mat.

2. Cut $1/4$-inch (.6-cm) strip off of the 12-inch (30.5-cm) side of red craft foam with
   regular scissors. Put this strip aside for later. Cut a large circle out of the remaining red craft foam. Then cut another circle out of the middle of the large circle,
   leaving a $1/2$-inch (1.3-cm) ring. Glue the ring onto the center of the place mat.

3. Cut letters to spell the word "LYING" out of the black craft foam. (Optional:
   Trace letter stencils on foam and then cut out letters.) Glue letters in order
   inside the red ring. Glue the $1/4$-inch (.6-cm) red strip you saved across the
   word "LYING" from one side of the ring to the other. Trim red strip to
   fit circle.

4. Let everything dry completely before using place mat. The place mat can
   remind you to tell the truth!

Getting Active

What You Need

markers

index cards

children's music CD and player

stopwatch or watch with a second hand

What You Do

1. **Let's play a game to celebrate the fact that we can ask God to forgive us for not telling the truth.** Print the word "forgive" on index cards, one letter on each card. Make at least one set of cards for every three to six children. Mix up all cards and place them facedown in a large circle on the floor.

2. Children form teams of three to six children. Assign a name or number to each team. Members from all teams stand in mixed-up order around the circle of cards.

3. As you play music, children walk around the circle. Stop the music after 15 to 20 seconds. When the music stops, each child picks up the card closest to him or her and finds other team members. Team members compare cards collected, keeping cards with letters needed to spell "forgive" and placing duplicate cards facedown back in the circle. Add blank cards to the circle as needed so that there is always a card for each child.

4. When one or more teams have collected a complete set of cards to spell "forgive," ask one or more children to answer the question, **When is a time kids your age can choose to tell the truth?**

Faith Builders at Home

Parents: Use these ideas to help build your child's faith, encouraging your child to become a lifelong follower of Jesus Christ.

"The Lord detests lying lips, but he delights in men who are truthful."
Proverbs 12:22

Key Word

Lying: Saying something on purpose that is not true.

Quick Pick

Read James 3:2-10 together to find out how important it is to use our words in good and honest ways.

Steppin' Out

Play an honesty add-on game together as a family. Begin the game by saying, "This week I can be honest when I (give the grocery clerk the extra change he or she gives me by mistake)." The next family member continues the game by saying how the first person can be honest and then adds on a time he or she can be honest (turn in money to the lost and found at school, tell the coach the truth about who kicked the ball out of bounds, etc.). See how long you can keep the game going!

Fun at Home

With your family, write on separate index cards five or six questions about Proverbs 12:22 and about telling the truth (What does the word "detest" mean? Who does God delight in? What might happen if you tell a lie to your friend and the friend finds out?). Also write five or six questions about your family (Where did we go for vacation last year? What is dad's favorite kind of ice cream? What TV show does [James] always watch?). Mix up the cards and put them facedown in a pile. Get a bell or rhythm instrument. One person chooses the top card and reads the question aloud. The first person to ring the bell or play the instrument answers the question and is given 100 points. Continue until questions have been answered.

Learning God's Ways

Lesson 26
Freedom in Christ

"You have been set free from sin and have become slaves to God, the benefit you reap leads to holiness, and the result is eternal life." Romans 6:22

Key Word

Freedom: To be able to choose what you do and say.

Opening Up

It's fun to celebrate holidays! Most countries have a holiday on which they celebrate their country's freedom. What is this holiday called? What do you like to do on this holiday?

Checking Out God's Word

When we have freedom, it means we can choose our words and actions.

- What are some of the actions we are free to do in our country?

The Bible tells us about a special freedom that the members of God's family have no matter what country they live in. Have a child read Romans 6:22 aloud.

- What do you think it means to be free from sin? Do you think it means members of God's family will never sin again? Why or why not?

- What is the reward we receive when we are members of God's family and free from sin?

This verse is good news for us because it tells us that we are no longer slaves to sin—we're free from sin. Members of God's family have God's help so that

they can choose to do right things. We can live in ways that show our love and obedience for God and serve Him—just like a slave serves his or her master.

- What good things can kids your age do to obey God?

- What can you do to learn more about what it means to be free from sin?

- When do you need God's help to obey Him?

Talking to God

If you have never chosen to be free from sin and be a member of God's family, you can do that today. If you are a member of God's family, you can thank Him for the freedom He gives you and ask His help in serving Him by your words and actions. Lead children in prayer. **Dear God, thank You for the freedom we have in our country. Thank You for the freedom You give us when we become members of Your family. We want to show our love for You by serving you. In Jesus' name, amen.**

Getting Crafty
Flag Puzzle

What Each Child Needs

newspaper

several tiny wooden stars

paintbrush

red, white and blue acrylic paints

seven craft sticks

craft glue

resealable sandwich bag

optional—star stickers instead of wooden
   stars

What Each Child Does

1. Cover work area with newspaper. Paint wooden stars white. (Note: To make flags
   from other countries, provide appropriate wooden shapes and colors of paint and
   modify the following instructions.) Set aside to dry.

2. Paint two craft sticks half blue and half red. Paint two craft sticks half blue and half
   white. Paint two craft sticks all red and one stick all white.

3. Line up the craft sticks to form a flag background. Glue the white stars onto the
   blue parts of the craft sticks. (Optional: Attach star stickers.) Make sure to glue
   stars to only one craft stick at a time, so the sticks can still be taken apart like a
   puzzle. Do not glue stars to overlap onto more than one craft stick.

4. Let everything dry completely. Keep your puzzle pieces in a sandwich bag.

5. Have fun with your puzzle at a holiday celebration.

Getting Active

What You Need

Bible

small index card

marker

children's music CD and player

What You Do

1. Print the words of Romans 6:22 on a small index card. Think of a question which can be answered by the information given in the verse.

2. Children stand in a circle (shoulder-to-shoulder if possible) to play a game similar to "Button, button, who's got the button?" Choose one child to be "It." "It" stands in the middle of the circle and closes eyes. Give the verse card to a child in the circle. (Optional: If you have a large group of children, make more than one verse card for children to pass.) "It" opens eyes.

3. As you play music, children pass card around the circle behind their backs, trying to keep "It" from seeing who has the card. When you stop the music, "It" tries to identify who has the card by asking a child the question you prepared. If the child does not have the card he or she answers, "Keep searching," and "It" asks another child. If the child does have the card, he or she answers by reading Romans 6:22 from the card. Child with the card becomes "It." Continue game as time permits.

Faith Builders at Home

Parents: Use these ideas to help build your child's faith, encouraging your child to become a lifelong follower of Jesus Christ.

> "You have been set free from sin and have become slaves to God, the benefit you reap leads to holiness, and the result is eternal life." Romans 6:22

Key Word

Freedom: To be able to choose what you do and say.

Quick Pick

On the Internet or at your local library, read about the beginning of the holiday on which your country celebrates freedom. Have your child tell one new thing he or she learned about the holiday. Thank God together for your country.

Steppin' Out

Start a new tradition in your family. Mark on a calendar the dates when family members chose to become members of God's family. Celebrate the dates by enjoying cake and ice cream to commemorate the freedom you have as members of God's family.

Fun at Home

Use poster board and markers to design a flag to represent the freedom we have in God. Use stripes, stars, crosses, hearts and/or other symbols. Put up the flag as a reminder of God's gift of freedom.

Learning God's Ways

Lesson 27
Hang in There!

"Blessed is the man who perseveres under trial, because when he has stood the test, he will receive the crown of life that God has promised to those who love him." James 1:12

Key Word

Persevere: To keep doing what's right, even when things get difficult.

Opening Up

When have you won a game? How did you feel when you won? Invite children to respond. **When have you lost a game? How did you feel? Did you want to play another game? Why or why not?** Invite children to respond.

Checking Out God's Word

Sometimes when a game is hard, or when we've lost a game, it's hard to keep on playing. It takes perseverance to win. Perseverance means to keep on doing something, even when it's hard. Living as a follower of God and doing what's right can take a lot of perseverance. Listen to what God says about someone who perseveres. Have a child read James 1:12 aloud.

■ **What does this verse say about someone who perseveres?**

■ **Why is it important not to give up when things get hard?**

■ **What kinds of situations make it hard for a kid your age to keep on doing what's right and obeying God?**

Each of us have times when we need God's help to keep doing what's right. God understands how we feel, and He promises to help us. God also promises that the people who don't give up will receive the "crown of life." That means the person who perseveres and loves God will get to live with Him forever!

Talking to God

Ask children to think about times when they need God's help to continue doing what's right. Invite volunteers to share their prayer requests. As each volunteer shares a request, ask someone to pray this week for the child. Then lead children in prayer, thanking God for His promise of help when we find it difficult to keep on doing what's right. Allow time for children to pray for each other.

Getting Crafty
"Hang in There" Picture Hanger

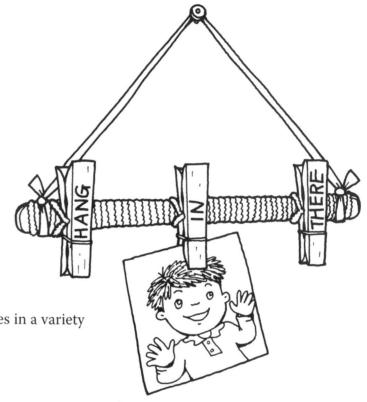

What Each Child Needs

tape

three craft sticks

approximately 15 chenille wires in a variety
  of colors

scissors

three spring-type clothespins

18-inch (45.5-cm) length of ribbon

What Each Child Does

1. With an adult's help, tape three craft sticks together to form one long stick. Do this by overlapping craft sticks about 1/2-inch (1.3-cm) and wrapping tape around sticks to secure in place.

2. Wrap chenille wires tightly around the long stick to create a colorful pattern.

3. Cut a chenille wire in half for each clothespin. Thread both pieces of chenille wire through the metal hole in the clothespin. Repeat for each clothespin. Twist the chenille wire around the long stick to secure each clothespin in place. Write "Hang in There" on the clothespins, with one word on each clothespin.

4. Tie one end of ribbon to one end of the long stick. Repeat on the other side with the other end of ribbon to create a hanger.

5. Hang up photographs or artwork by clipping them with the clothespins. The hanger will remind you and others to "Hang in There."

Getting Active

What You Need

masking tape

materials for one of the activities listed below

What You Do

1. **In order to persevere, we may need to practice something over and over again. The more we practice something, the better we'll become at it. Let's practice some things several times to see how long we can persevere.** Set up one or more of the activities below.

2. Explain activities to the children. Children move around to the different activities as time allows. Make sure children try the chosen activity more than once so that they get to practice it.

Beanbag Toss

Set a large plastic bowl or tub about 5 feet (1.5 m) from a masking-tape line. Children stand behind line, face away from tub and toss beanbag over shoulder back toward the tub.

Marshmallow Move

Set an open bag of marshmallows and a pair of chopsticks 4 feet (1.2 m) from a plastic bowl. Children use chopsticks to pick up a marshmallow and carry it to the plastic bowl without touching marshmallow with their hands.

Faith Builders at Home

Parents: Use these ideas to help build your child's faith, encouraging your child to become a lifelong follower of Jesus Christ.

"Blessed is the man who perseveres under trial, because when he has stood the test, he will receive the crown of life that God has promised to those who love him." James 1:12

Key Word

Persevere: To keep doing what's right, even when things get difficult.

Fun at Home

Have a storytelling night at your home. Invite your child's friends to your home. Find a story in a newspaper or magazine about someone who persevered during a difficult time. Tell the story to your child and his or her friends. Then read the story of Daniel in Daniel 6 and compare the two examples of people who kept doing what was right.

Steppin' Out

Go to a running track at a local high school or community recreation center. Walk or jog around the track as many times as you can. Discuss how athletes must learn to persevere even when they feel like giving up. Enjoy a cold drink after the exercise. Thank God together for His help in strengthening your family to keep doing what's right.

Quick Pick

Have each family member write on a separate sheet of paper a way in which he or she wishes to persevere in doing what's right this week. Put the papers in envelopes and seal them. Label the envelopes with the person's name. Pray for each other, asking God to help each person obey God. Collect the envelopes. At the end of the week, give each person his or her envelope to open and read to see if he or she was able to fulfill his or her plan.

Learning God's Ways

Lesson 28
Humility

> "Do nothing out of selfish ambition or vain conceit, but in humility consider others better than yourselves." Philippians 2:3

Key Word

Humility: To think of others before yourself, instead of being selfish.

Opening Up

What kind of awards do kids your age receive? When have you gotten an award from a coach or a teacher? How did getting the award and being the center of attention make you feel? Children tell responses.

Checking Out God's Word

It makes us feel good to receive awards, and most of us like being the center of attention! But have you ever been around someone who wanted to receive ALL the awards and wanted to be the center of attention ALL the time?

■ How do kids usually feel about people who want all the attention?

■ When might a kid your age think that he or she is better than everyone else?

The Bible says something interesting about the way we should think of ourselves and how we should treat others. Have a child read Philippians 2:3 aloud.

■ How does someone who is selfish treat others?

■ What does Philippians 2:3 say we should do instead of being selfish or conceited?

When we're humble, it means we don't think we deserve all the attention. The Bible tells us how humble people treat others. Read Philippians 2:4 aloud.

■ What are ways that kids can show that they care about the feelings and needs of others, instead of just caring about themselves?

Talking to God

Before we pray today, think of someone you see every day or at least once a week. You might think of your parents, a brother or sister, a friend, a teacher or a player on your (baseball) team. Allow children several moments to think of people. **Now think of one way to show that you care about the feelings and needs of the person you thought of.** Invite volunteers to tell their responses. Then lead children in prayer. **Dear God, thank You for loving us. Help us to show Your love and be humble in the ways we treat others. In Jesus' name, amen.**

Getting Crafty
Verse Pouch

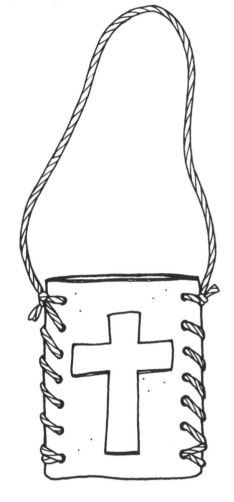

What Each Child Needs

Bible

4x12-inch (10x30.5-cm) piece
    of craft foam

hole punch

tape

1 yard (.9 m) length of yarn

craft foam scraps or shapes

index card

marker

What Each Child Does

1. Fold the piece of craft foam in half. Punch holes every $1/2$-inch (1.3-cm) down
    both sides of the folded craft foam. Do not punch hole in the top of the craft
    foam or on the folded edge.

2. Wrap a small piece of tape around the tip of one end of the yarn to make it easier
    to thread through the punched holes. Thread yarn through the holes on one side
    of the pouch. Tie off the ends. Repeat step on the other side of the pouch. Use
    remainder of yarn to tie a strap from one side of pouch to the other side.

3. Glue craft foam scraps or pre-cut designs as decorations on the front of pouch.

4. Write Philippians 2:3 on the index card and put it inside the pouch. (Optional:
    Provide additional index cards on which children can write other verses to keep
    in the pouch.)

Getting Active

What You Need

large container

index cards

soft balls or beanbags

marker

What You Do

1. **God will help us be humble in the way we treat others so that we can show His love to them. Let's try doing that in our game today!** Place the container on the floor on one side of the playing area.

2. Group the children into teams of six to eight. Teams line up single file about 5 feet (1.5 m) from the container. Give each child an index card. Give the first child on each team a ball or beanbag.

3. Stand near the container with the marker in your hand. Children from each team take turns tossing the ball or beanbag into the container. Each time a child gets the ball or beanbag into the container, print one letter of the word "humble" on his or her index card.

4. When a child gets all the letters for the word, he or she continues taking turns, giving any letters scored to the next person in line. Continue until all children have "humble" written on their cards.

Faith Builders at Home

Parents: Use these ideas to help build your child's faith, encouraging your child to become a lifelong follower of Jesus Christ.

"Do nothing out of selfish ambition or vain conceit, but in humility consider others better than yourselves." Philippians 2:3

Key Word

Humility: To think of others before yourself, instead of being selfish.

Fun at Home

Make a Humble Hands poster. Trace around each other's hands on a large sheet of paper. Family members write on their hands ways to be humble and think of the needs of others.

Quick Pick

Give each person in your family an index card and a marker. Tape the index card somewhere on the front of each person's body. Have each family member write one thing another person is good at on that person's index card. Help your child identify his or her strengths and abilities. Tell your family that God has made each person unique. End the activity by thanking God for each person and his or her unique talents.

Steppin' Out

Find or buy an interesting hat. Call it the "Humility Hat." Place the hat upside down on the floor. Each person takes a turn to toss a coin into the hat. When a coin lands in the hat, the person who tossed the coin puts on the hat and tells a way to care about the feelings and needs of others. (Optional: Person says the words of Philippians 2:3 or 2:4.)

Learning God's Ways

Lesson 29
Joy

> "Be joyful always."
> 1 Thessalonians 5:16

Key Word

Joy: To be happy in all situations.

Opening Up

How many different things can you think of that make you happy? Choose several children to respond.

Checking Out God's Word

It would be great if we could be happy all the time every day! On some days, however, we don't feel so happy. Listen to what the Bible says we should do when we're not so happy. Read 1 Thessalonians 5:16 aloud.

■ **What does this verse say we should be? When?**

■ **Why can people who are in God's family be joyful, even when they don't feel happy?**

God understands that sometimes we might feel sad, disappointed or worried. But even in those times, we can have joy because of God's love for us. God loves us so much that He promises to be with us and help us, even in difficult situations. Have a child read 1 Thessalonians 5:17-18 aloud.

■ **When might kids your age find it hard to have joy?**

■ **What can we do when we don't feel happy and we need joy?**

■ **What can we do to show that we remember God's greatness and love?**

Our joy comes from knowing that God always loves and cares for us. Every day and in every situation, we can thank God for the great things He has done for us and ask Him for joy.

Talking to God

Let's pray and thank God for the great things He has done. Let's ask Him to help us have joy, too! Lead children in prayer, inviting volunteers to either thank God for His greatness or ask Him for joy. End the prayer time by praying, **Dear God, You are awesome! Thank You for always loving and caring for us. Help us to have joy by remembering all the wonderful things You've done for us. In Jesus' name, amen.**

Getting Crafty
Joyful Centerpiece

What Each Child Needs

silver or gold paint

paintbrush

2-inch (5-cm) clay pot

silver or gold curling ribbon

scissors

tape

$5/8$-inch (1.59-cm) wooden dowel

plaster of paris

water

4-inch (10-cm) piece of craft foam

glue

silver or gold glitter

What Each Child Does

1. Paint the clay pot silver or gold. Set it aside to dry.

2. Cut 40 pieces of ribbon about 6 inches (15 cm) long. Lay a 2-inch (5-cm) piece of tape on a flat surface with the sticky side up. Place one end of a piece of ribbon on the tape so it sticks. Add six or seven pieces of ribbon to the tape. Make sure that the ribbons are curling up from the flat surface.

3. Wrap the tape with ribbon on it around the middle of the wooden dowel. Make as many strips of tape with ribbon as you like. Keep adding tape with ribbon to the dowel to create layers of sparkle.

4. With an adult's help, mix $1/2$ cup (120 ml) of plaster of paris as directed on the package. Place a small piece of tape over the hole in the bottom of the clay pot. Pour the plaster into the pot. When the plaster has begun to thicken, push the wooden dowel vertically into the center of the pot.

5. Cut any shape out of the craft foam. With glue, write the word "JOY" on the craft foam shape and sprinkle with glitter. Glue craft foam shape to the top of the wooden dowel.

6. Place the centerpiece on a table or in a window as a reminder of the joy God gives us.

Getting Active

What You Need

construction paper

marker

masking tape

What You Do

1. **God has done so many great things for which we can worship Him! Let's play a game where we joyfully remember the great things He's done for us.** Print the following gifts from God on separate sheets of construction paper: forgiveness, family, prayer, love, courage, talents, salvation, Jesus, power. Use masking tape to make a life-sized Tic-Tac-Toe grid in the playing area. Place one paper, words face-down, in each section of the grid.

2. Divide group into two equal teams. Assign one team X and the other team O. Volunteers from each team take turns choosing sections of the grid to stand in with arms in X or O shapes (see sketch). Teams continue taking turns until one team has three students standing in a row or until all sections of the grid are occupied.

3. Invite a volunteer from the winning team (or the team who had the last turn) to choose one of the papers on which a team member is standing. That team member turns the paper over and reads the words aloud. Then a volunteer tells a way in which he or she can joyfully praise God for that gift (sing a song, say a prayer, etc.).

4. Repeat game as time permits, volunteers turning over different cards at the end of each round.

Faith Builders at Home

Parents: Use these ideas to help build your child's faith, encouraging your child to become a lifelong follower of Jesus Christ.

"Be joyful always."
1 Thessalonians 5:16

Key Word

Joy: To be happy in all situations.

Steppin' Out

Ask each member of your family to name one or two things your family does together that makes him or her happy. Thank God together for the good things He helps us enjoy. Then each week choose one activity for your family to do. Mark your plans on a calendar.

Quick Pick

Joy is one of the Fruits of the Spirit. Read about the other Fruits of the Spirit in Galatians 5:22-23. Ask each family member to choose one of the fruits listed in these verses and tell a way to show that fruit at home, school or work.

Fun at Home

Music is a great way to show joy for what God has done. Play an upbeat praise song during a meal or while you are driving in the car. (Optional: See how many household items you can find to keep time to the music—tap spoons together, beat on an upside down pan, shake a bag of uncooked pasta, etc.)

Sharing Jesus with Others

Lesson 30
Going Fishing

> " 'Come, follow me,' Jesus said, 'and I will make you fishers of men.' "
> Matthew 4:19
>
> ### Key Word
>
> Disciple: Someone who follows the teachings and example of another.

Opening Up

Have you ever been fishing? If so, tell us about your experience. Where did you go? What kind of bait did you use? Did you catch anything? Invite children to respond. Imagine that you were going on a fishing trip. What kind of things would you bring with you?

Checking Out God's Word

In Bible times, many people fished to provide for their families. They would sell the fish they caught to others in nearby villages. One day, Jesus met some of these fishermen. Let's find out what happened. Have a child read Matthew 4:18-22 aloud.

■ What did Jesus say to the fishermen?

Jesus saw the fishermen and asked them to follow Him. Jesus told them He would make them "fishers of men." The fishermen left their boat and their father to follow Jesus.

■ What do you think Jesus meant by saying "fishers of men?"

■ If getting people to follow Jesus is like fishing, how do you think you "catch" them?

When Jesus said that He would make us fishers of men, He meant that He would help others learn about Him by what we say and do. Then more people can become disciples of Jesus. The fishermen stopped their fishing and followed Jesus so that they could become fishers of men.

■ What can you say and do to help others learn about Jesus?

Talking to God

Let's pray together that the things we say and do will help others learn about Jesus. Lead children in prayer.

Getting Crafty
Fishing Game

What Each Child Needs

12-inch (30.5-cm) wooden dowel

24 inches (61 cm) of yarn

craft glue

2 small round magnets

scissors

craft foam in various colors

glitter

sparkle sequins

permanent markers

jumbo paper clips

What Each Child Does

1. Wrap one end of the yarn around one end of the dowel several times and tie it tightly. (Optional: For more security, apply a thin layer of craft glue to the dowel before wrapping the yarn.)

2. Place the other end of the yarn in between the two magnets and glue together like a sandwich. Set the completed rod aside to dry.

3. Cut out fish shapes from the colored craft foam to create foam shapes for decoration. Glue glitter and sparkle sequins. Or draw faces or designs on shapes with permanent markers. (Optional: Instead of making fish shapes, make other sea creatures like starfish, seahorses, octopus, etc.)

4. Poke a jumbo paper clip through the mouth of each fish. (Optional: Children use fishing poles to participate in a contest to see who can catch a fish the fastest.)

Getting Active

What You Need

masking tape

What You Do

1. On the floor, use masking tape to form at least three shapes large enough to fit the number of children in your group. (For example, if you have 20 children, make four squares or rectangles large enough for five children to stand in each shape.)

2. Ask a child to be "It." Form three groups from remaining children. Each group stands in a separate shape marked on the floor.

3. One at a time call out descriptions with the word "disciples." For example, "disciples wearing blue" or "disciples wearing tennis shoes." Children who fit each description run to new shapes while "It" tries to tag them before they are inside their new shapes. Any child who is tagged becomes "It" also. Continue play, periodically calling out "Switcheroo" at which all children must run to new shapes. When only a few children have not been tagged, begin a new round of the game. Begin the new round with a new "It."

Faith Builders at Home

Parents: Use these ideas to help build your child's faith, encouraging your child to become a lifelong follower of Jesus Christ.

> " 'Come, follow me,' Jesus said, 'and I will make you fishers of men.' "
> Matthew 4:19
>
> ## Key Word
>
> **Disciple: Someone who follows the teachings and example of another.**

Steppin' Out

Take a fishing trip to a nearby lake or pond. See how many types of fish you can catch! No lake nearby? Take a visit to your nearest pet store to see the different varieties of fish God made.

Quick Pick

Play a game of "Follow the Leader." Discuss how being a disciple of Jesus means that we are followers of Jesus.

Fun at Home

Make a wordless book. Cut and staple together five small pieces of paper. Color one page yellow to represent God's wonderful creation of the world and you. Then color a page gray for sin that separates us from God, a page red for Jesus who died for us, a page purple for eternal life and a page green for growing in Christ as His disciple. Have your child explain to you and/or a friend what each page means.

Sharing Jesus with Others

Lesson 31
Looking for Sheep

> "I am the good shepherd. The good shepherd lays down his life for the sheep."
> John 10:11

Key Word

Search: To look carefully to find something.

Opening Up

Have you ever lost something that was important to you? How did you feel? How did you try to find what you lost? If you found what you lost, what was your reaction when you found it? Invite children to respond.

Checking Out God's Word

In the Bible, Jesus tells us a story about losing something special. Let's find out what was lost. Read Luke 15:3-7 aloud.

■ What was lost in this story? How was it found?

Jesus tells us about lost sheep in this story. Jesus used the example of sheep to represent people. Jesus refers to people who are not His followers as lost sheep. Because Jesus loves and cares for everyone, He is like a shepherd who takes special care of sheep.

■ What does Jesus say the shepherd does when he finds the missing sheep?

The shepherd celebrates when a lost sheep has been found. In that same way, Jesus celebrates when a person chooses to love and follow Him. Read John 10:11 aloud.

■ What are some ways we can help others learn about Jesus and how He is like a shepherd who loves them?

Talking to God

Let's pray and thank Jesus for loving and caring for us like a shepherd cares for his sheep. Give each child a slip of paper and pencil. Each child writes his or her name on the paper. Collect papers and put them in a small container. Children take turns choosing papers, making sure they don't choose their own names. Each child prays "Thank You Jesus, for being (Kelli's) shepherd and for loving (her)." End the prayer time by asking God's help in telling others about Jesus' love.

Getting Crafty
Lost Sheep Game

What Each Child Needs

air drying clay or play dough

4 plastic or paper cups

glue

water

paintbrush

2-inch (5-cm) squares of fabric

What Each Child Does

1. With an adult's help, mold a small sheep out of clay and set it aside to dry. Make sure that it is small enough to fit under an upside-down cup.

2. In one cup, mix equal parts glue and water. Use this mixture and a paintbrush to glue the fabric squares on the outside of the three remaining cups. (Optional: To make cups look like green hills, use green fabric or fabric printed with leaves or other plant patterns.)

3. Allow the sheep and the cups to dry completely.

4. To play game, you'll need at least two people. Place the three decorated cups upside-down on a table. Hide the clay sheep under one of the cups and rearrange cup order. One person guesses which cup the lost sheep is under.

Getting Active

What You Do

1. **Let's play a game to remind us of a shepherd's love for lost sheep.** Children form two teams. Children on each team take off shoes and place them in a team pile on one side of the playing area. Children line up in single-file lines on other side of playing area, across from their team's shoe pile. Mix up shoes within each pile.

2. At your signal, the first child on each team skips to shoe pile, finds one of his or her "lost" shoes, puts it on and skips back to his or her team. The next child in line repeats the action. Children continue, taking turns until everyone on team has found their "lost" shoes.

Faith Builders at Home

Parents: Use these ideas to help build your child's faith, encouraging your child to become a lifelong follower of Jesus Christ.

"I am the good shepherd. The good shepherd lays down his life for the sheep."
John 10:11

Key Word

Search: To look carefully to find something.

Steppin' Out

Find out about missionaries your church supports who are helping "lost sheep" come to know Jesus. During the week, find ways to help your child earn money to send to a missionary (collect loose change, bake and sell cookies, do an extra chore, etc.).

Quick Pick

Talk about how Jesus is like a loving shepherd who searches for lost sheep (people who don't follow Him). Take turns hiding an object in your house for others to find. Then pray together thanking Jesus for being like a loving shepherd.

Fun at Home

Using a video camera or digital camera, act out and record the parable in Luke 15:3-7 to show God's love and joy for His sheep.

Sharing Jesus with Others

Lesson 32
Light of the World

> "You are the light of the world."
> Matthew 5:14

Key Word

Light: Something that helps you see in the dark.

Opening Up

How would our lives be different if we had no lights except the sun and moon? Invite children to tell ideas.

Checking Out God's Word

Light allows us to see things that we would not be able to see. Jesus explains to us in the Bible why we are like lights. Read Matthew 5:14-16 aloud.

■ **How are we like lights for God?**

■ **Why do you think Jesus tells us to "let our light shine before men?"**

When we obey God with our words and actions, we are like lights to the people around us. If people begin to see how much we love and obey God, then they will begin to love and obey Him too. God wants others to see the good things He has done for us so that they may learn more about Him.

■ **Which of these could you see better on a dark night: a flashlight shining in a sleeping bag or a flashlight shining straight up in the sky?**

■ Read Matthew 5:15 aloud. **Do you think it is easier to see with a light under a bowl or on a stand? Why?**

If you cover a light, it is harder to see. Jesus tells us to put our light on a stand so that it may give light to everyone.

■ **What is something you can do to show others how much you love and obey God?**

Talking to God

Let's ask God to help us love and obey Him with our words and actions so we can be like lights to help others see God. Lead children in prayer.

Getting Crafty
Light of the World Candle

What Each Child Needs

clean, dry baby food jar

small stickers

paintbrush

glue

glitter

ribbon

tea light candle

What Each Child Does

1. Place stickers on the outside of the jar.

2. Use a paintbrush to spread a very thick layer of glue over the entire outside surface of the jar, covering the stickers. Sprinkle glitter lightly over the outside of the jar and shake off the excess.

3. Tie a ribbon around the top of the jar and place the tea light candle inside. (Optional: To make larger candles, use mason jars and votive candles.)

Getting Active

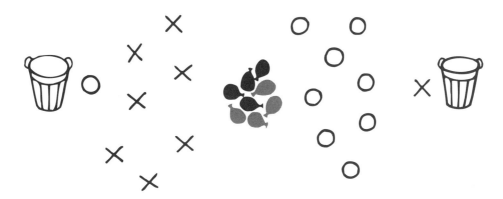

What You Need

balloons in two colors

plastic garbage bag

two large boxes or garbage cans

What You Do

1. **Jesus teaches us to live in ways that show we love and obey Him. Let's play a game like soccer. Your actions will show which team you're on. Let's also see if your attitude when you play can show that you belong to Jesus.**

2. Inflate and tie balloons, an equal number of each color. (Prepare one balloon for each child. If you have a small group, prepare more than one balloon for each child.) Place balloons in garbage bag for storage.

3. Play a game similar to soccer, using multiple balloons. Place balloons on the floor in the middle of a large playing area. Children form two teams. Assign each team a balloon color and choose a child from each team to be a scorer. Scorer stands behind the opposing team, in front of a large box or garbage can (see sketch).

4. At your signal, all team members try to kick balloons of their team's color to their scorer. Scorer grabs his or her team's balloons and puts them into the box or can. After several minutes of play, call time. Team with most balloons in the box or can wins.

Faith Builders at Home

Parents: Use these ideas to help build your child's faith, encouraging your child to become a lifelong follower of Jesus Christ.

"You are the light of the world."
Matthew 5:14

Key Word

Light: Something that helps you see in the dark.

Quick Pick

Before bedtime, darken your child's bedroom and ask him or her to complete a task in the room (clean up games or books, get out pajamas, hang up clothes, etc.). Then turn on the lights and ask your child to complete a similar task. Talk with your child about how helpful light is and how our actions can be like lights in helping others see how to love and obey God.

Fun at Home

Collect a flashlight. Have each family member sit in a circle in a dark room. Turn the flashlight on, place it on a hard surface and spin it around. The person on whom the flashlight is shining when it stops spinning tells one way to be a light for God to others.

Steppin' Out

From the Internet or a library book, find a chart that shows the names and positions of a variety of stars and/or constellations. Take a star walk together and see how many stars and/or constellations you can see. As part of the walk, pray together, asking God's help in being like lights that help others see how to love and obey God.

Sharing Jesus with Others

Lesson 33
Sharing with Others

> "And do not forget to do good and to share with others."
> Hebrews 13:16

Key Word

Share: To give part of something you have to someone else.

Opening Up

What is something you have shared with someone in your family? What would be the most important thing you could share with a friend or family member? Why? Invite children to respond.

Checking Out God's Word

We can share many things with one another. Some of us share food, toys and some of us even share rooms at our homes! When we share, it means that we give something we know or have to someone else. Today we'll read about a follower of Jesus named Andrew who shared something very important with his brother. Read John 1:35-42 aloud.

■ In verse 41, what did Andrew tell his brother, Simon Peter?

■ Why do you think Andrew chose to find his brother first and tell him about Jesus?

The first thing Andrew did after spending time with Jesus was tell his brother about Jesus. Andrew shared the good news that he had found Jesus and brought Simon Peter to see Jesus. Read Hebrews 13:16 aloud.

■ What did Jesus say when He met Simon Peter?

■ Do you think that Simon Peter would have met Jesus if Andrew hadn't brought him to Jesus? Why or why not?

■ Who has shared the good news of Jesus with you? Who can you share the news about Jesus with?

Talking to God

It's important to know that we can share Jesus' love with others just like we share other things with each other. Let's pray and ask God for His help in sharing Jesus' love with others. Lead children in prayer.

Getting Crafty
Cloth Strip Picture Frame

What Each Child Needs

inexpensive wooden or cardboard
  picture frame

glue

water

plastic bowl

mixing spoon

sponge brush

1x12-inch (2.5x30.5-cm) strips of
  colorful fabric

duct tape

photograph of a family member

What Each Child Does

1. Take the picture frame apart and set aside the back of the frame. If there is glass, discard it safely.

2. In the bowl, mix one part water with two parts glue to form watery glue.

3. Using the sponge brush, apply glue to the front of a small portion of the picture frame. Wrap one fabric strip around the frame (going through the center hole), adding more glue as needed.

4. Continue this process, adding glue and strips of fabric until the frame is completely wrapped. Glue the ends of the fabric strips to hold them in place.

5. Place a photograph of a family member in the frame so the picture shows through the opening. Replace back of frame and secure with duct tape if needed.

6. Keep the photo in a special place in your room. Use it as a reminder to pray for the person in the photo.

Getting Active

What You Need

Bible

two large rubber balls or tennis balls

permanent marker or masking tape

children's music CD and player

What You Do

1. Write "1" on one ball and "2" on the other ball (numbers may be formed with masking tape if needed). Children stand in a circle and practice bouncing the ball to each other.

2. Ask a child to read Hebrews 13:16 aloud. **What does this verse command us to do?** (Share with others. Do good.) **What are some ways to follow these commands?** Children tell ideas.

3. When you start the music, children begin bouncing the balls to each other. When you stop the music, children holding balls name that many ways to obey Hebrews 13:16.

Faith Builders at Home

Parents: Use these ideas to help build your child's faith, encouraging your child to become a lifelong follower of Jesus Christ.

"I tell you the truth, whatever you did for one of the least of these brothers of mine, you did for me." Matthew 25:40

Key Word

Care: To express genuine interest or concern.

Fun at Home

With your family, pass a slice of bread to each person. Each person tears off a piece of bread and tells one way to share the love of Jesus with others. Once everyone has a piece of bread, pray and ask God for His help to care for others. Everyone eats his or her bread. (Just for fun—try a different variety of bread than you usually eat!)

Steppin' Out

As a family, share Jesus' love by preparing some snack bags for children at a homeless center. Decorate the bags with markers and stickers and then fill with juice boxes, granola bars and fruit snacks. (Optional: In each bag, include a pencil, a small rubber ball or a comic book.)

Quick Pick

Help your child plan a sharing day with a friend. Have your child invite a friend over and plan to share a special toy, movie or game.

Sharing Jesus with Others

Lesson 34
Being Bold

> "Don't let anyone look down on you because you are young, but set an example for the believers in speech, in life, in love, in faith and in purity." 1 Timothy 4:12

Key Word

Bold: To show courage.

Opening Up

Have you ever been told that you were too young to do something? Tell something you wish you could do if you were older. Invite children to tell ideas.

Checking Out God's Word

Sometimes people may think that you can't do certain things because of your age. The Bible tells us something that you can do no matter how old you are. Have a child read 1 Timothy 4:12 aloud.

- **Why do you think some older people might look down on younger people?**

- **What does this verse say you can be an example of?**

The Bible tells us that even though you may be young, you can be an example to others by the way you live and act.

You can be courageous in the things you say and do that show how much you love and obey God. When you show courage, it means you are being bold.

- **Why do you think God says that kids your age can be an example to others?**

- **What are some things kids your age can do to be good examples for others?**

Talking to God

Lead children in prayer. Pray for each child by name, asking God's help in boldly being good examples. (Optional: Children sit in a circle. Open the prayer time by saying, **Dear God, please help each child be bold examples of ways to love and obey You. We pray for. . . ."** Let each child say the name of child sitting to his or her right.)

Getting Crafty
Growing Bolder Chart

What Each Child Needs

scissors

measuring tape

stapler

24x36-inch (61x91.5-cm) any color
  butcher paper

glue

letter stencils in a variety of colors

markers

What Each Child Does

1. With an adult's help, cut measuring tape at the 36-inch (91.5-cm) mark. Discard lower portion of measuring tape. Staple the remaining measuring tape along one side of the butcher paper to make growth chart.

2. Place the chart on a flat surface (if you don't have a big enough table, the floor works well). Glue stencils to chart to spell out "Don't let anyone think less of you because you are young."(Optional: Use stencils to trace and color letters to spell out phrase.) Decorate the rest of the poster chart using markers.

3. At home, find a blank wall to hang your chart on. (The back of a door can be a good place.) From the floor, measure up 36 inches (91.5 cm) on the wall. This is where the bottom of the chart should be attached (see sketch). (Optional: Make one chart for each group of six to eight children. Measure each person in the group. Have children write names and the date on the chart. Measure each person in the group every few months to record their growth during the next year.)

Getting Active

What You Need

index cards

pen or marker

hula hoops

What You Do

1. As a group, brainstorm ways to be an example in loving and obeying God. Write each way on a separate index card. Scatter the cards in your game-playing area.

2. Divide group into teams of three or four. Give each team a hula hoop. Team members step into the hoop. Each team member holds the hoop with one hand.

3. At your signal, teams quickly move through the area, using their free hands to pick up index cards. Teams see how many they can pick up in 30 seconds. Repeat as time permits.

Faith Builders at Home

Parents: Use these ideas to help build your child's faith, encouraging your child to become a lifelong follower of Jesus Christ.

"Don't let anyone look down on you because you are young, but set an example for the believers in speech, in life, in love, in faith and in purity." 1 Timothy 4:12

Key Word

Bold: To show courage.

Steppin' Out

As a family, look through one or two newspapers to find stories and/or pictures of people who are positive examples.

Quick Pick

Read a Bible story together about someone who was bold even though he was young (David and Goliath—1 Samuel 17; King Josiah—2 Chronicles 34; Meshach, Shadrach and Abednego—Daniel 3).

Fun at Home

Play a fun tossing game. Place a laundry basket or box on the floor. Each person stands with back to the container and takes a turn tossing a small or soft ball over his or her shoulder, trying to toss the ball into the container. When the ball lands in the container, player tells a way to obey 1 Timothy 4:12.

Getting Ready for School

Lesson 35
Friendship

> "A friend loves at all times."
> Proverbs 17:17

Key Word

Friend: Someone who you like being with and who you can depend on.

Opening Up

Name a good friend that you have. What is he or she like? What kinds of things do you like to do with your friend? Invite children to tell answers.

Checking Out God's Word

The Bible has something to say about the importance of friendship. Read Ecclesiastes 4:9-12 and see if you can find at least four reasons it is good to have friends.

■ **Verse 9 says that friends working together can get more done. When have you helped a friend with something that he or she needed to do?**

■ **Verse 10 says that friends can help each other up if they fall. When has a friend helped you through a tough time?**

■ **Verse 11 says that friends can help each other keep warm. When have you encouraged someone and made them feel good or "warm" on the inside?**

■ **Verse 12 says that friends can help defend each other. How might you help a friend fight off temptation and choose to do what is right?**

■ **Verse 12 mentions that a cord of three strands cannot be quickly broken. If one strand is you and one strand is your friend, who do you think the third strand is? Why do you think it's important to have friends who love Jesus?**

We've talked about a lot of ways to be good friends today. What can you do to be a better friend this year at school?

Talking to God

Let's pray that we will be the kind of friends described in the Bible. Read Proverbs 17:17 aloud. Lead children in prayer. **Dear God, thank You for giving us friends. Show us ways to help each other at all times. In Jesus' name, amen.**

Getting Crafty
Friendship Phone Books

What Each Child Needs

1 small spiral notebook

card stock in a variety of colors

ink pads of various colors

small alphabet rubber stamps

other decorative rubber stamps

scissors

glue sticks

optional—markers

What Each Child Does

1. Cut a piece of card stock to fit the front cover of your notebook. (Optional: For a more colorful look, cut a second piece of card stock slightly smaller than the first piece. Glue second piece of card stock on top of the first piece.)

2. Use alphabet rubber stamps to print "Friends' Phone Numbers" on the card stock cover. Use other decorative rubber stamps to decorate. (Optional: Use markers to print title and decorate.) Give the ink a few minutes to dry before you glue card stock cover to the front of the notebook. (Optional: Also cover the back cover with decorated card stock.)

3. Ask your friends to write their names and phone numbers in the book before you take it home. (Optional: Ask friends for birthdays if phone numbers are not available.) Take your book to school to get more names and phone numbers.

Getting Active

What You Need

balloon for each pair of children

large plastic bag

What You Do

1. **Friends can be helpful to us in many ways. Let's play a game where we need friends to help us carry balloons.** Inflate and tie the balloons. Place them in a large plastic bag.

2. Children form pairs. Pairs stand at one side of playing area. Give each pair a balloon. (Optional: For a greater challenge, children increase the number of balloons to carry.)

3. Pairs experiment with a variety of ways in which to carry the balloon to the other side of the playing area without using their hands to hold the balloon. For example, children may hold balloon between shoulders, heads or hips.

4. After children have had time to try several methods of carrying the balloon, ask all pairs to line up at one side of the playing area. Each pair chooses the method of carrying the balloon they think will be the fastest. At your signal, pairs carry balloons to the other side of the playing area and back, trying to see who can complete the task first.

Faith Builders at Home

Parents: Use these ideas to help build your child's faith, encouraging your child to become a lifelong follower of Jesus Christ.

> "A friend loves at all times."
> Proverbs 17:17
>
> ## Key Word
>
> **Friend: Someone who you like being with and who you can depend on.**

Quick Pick

Take turns completing the sentence "A good friend is someone who. . . ." See how many different sentences you can think of.

Steppin' Out

Have your child invite a friend over this week. Let your child and his or her friend use a camera to take pictures of each other (or you can take pictures of the two friends). Print an extra set of pictures for the friend, or if using a digital camera, send pictures to the friends' family.

Fun at Home

When you're at the store, purchase some neon markers or glitter pens. With your child, make posters illustrating Proverbs 17:17.

Getting Ready for School

Lesson 36
Sharing Generously

"You will be made rich in every way so that you can be generous on every occasion." 2 Corinthians 9:11

Key Word

Generosity: To be willing to give or share with others.

Opening Up

What is your favorite thing that you own? How would you feel if someone asked to borrow it? Would you let someone borrow it? Why or why not? Invite children to respond.

Checking Out God's Word

Being willing to share with others is not always easy. Let's find out what the Bible says about sharing. Read 2 Corinthians 9:11 aloud.

- What do you think is the main idea of this verse?

- What does God promise in this verse?

- Why do you think God wants us to be generous "on every occasion?"

Being generous does not mean to just give or share things with others; it also means to willingly share your time or abilities with others. For example, if a person in a wheelchair needs help opening a door, you can be generous and open the door. Or if a friend at school has a job to do, you can help with the job.

- How has someone shown generosity to you?

- When is a time you can show generosity to others?

- When is it easy to share generously? When is it hard?

Talking to God

Let's pray today for God's help in showing generosity to others. Lead children in prayer. **Dear God, thank You for being generous to us. Help us to show Your love by showing generosity to others. In Jesus' name, amen.** After prayer, have each child tell another child one way they will show generosity to someone else today.

Getting Crafty
Pencil Toppers

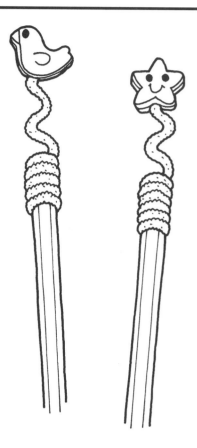

What Each Child Needs

variety of small wooden shapes

acrylic paint in various colors

fine-tipped paintbrushes

glue

2 new pencils

chenille wire in various colors

scissors

What Each Child Does

1. Choose two small wooden shapes and paint them. (Optional: Paint the back of the shapes.) Set aside to dry.

2. Apply a small layer of glue around the metal part of the eraser on the pencil. Wrap one end of a chenille wire several times tightly around the glued area. Extend the rest of the chenille wire beyond the end of the eraser and twist in a spiral shape.) Trim the chenille wire to the desired length.

3. Apply a small amount of glue to the back of the painted wooden shape and attach to the end of the chenille wire. Repeat steps 2 and 3 with the second pencil.

4. Keep one pencil topper for yourself and give one to a friend.

Getting Active

What You Need

individually wrapped snacks (at least one per child)

paper plates

What You Do

1. **Being willing to give to others is one way to show generosity. Let's play a game where we generously give snacks to each other.** Group children into teams of five to seven children each. Teams line up on one side of the classroom. Set an empty paper plate next to the first child on each team. Place a plate of snacks across the playing area from each team.

2. At your signal, the first child on each team walks quickly to the other side of the room, retrieves a snack from the team's plate and brings it back, placing it on the team's empty plate. The next child in line repeats the action, leaving as the first child places the snack on the plate. Play continues until all members on the team have collected a snack.

3. Each child takes a snack from the team's plate and gives it to someone else on the team. Children chew and swallow snacks, and then begin to whistle. First team to have all its team members whistling wins!

Faith Builders at Home

Parents: Use these ideas to help build your child's faith, encouraging your child to become a lifelong follower of Jesus Christ.

"You will be made rich in every way so that you can be generous on every occasion." 2 Corinthians 9:11

Key Word

Generosity: To be willing to give or share with others.

Quick Pick

Play a fun word game together. First player says the name of something he or she can share with others. Next player names something to share that begins with the last letter of the first item. Play continues until someone is stumped. Then begin a new round!

Fun at Home

On a large sheet of paper write the names of family members in a column down the left side of the paper. During the week, each time a family member does something generous for someone else, draw a star next to his or her name. At the end of the week, celebrate all the stars received by sharing a special snack together.

Steppin' Out

Purchase school supplies (pencils, crayons, markers, scissors, backpack, paper notebooks, etc.) for your family to give to a community organization that helps needy children.

Getting Ready for School

Lesson 37
Forgiveness

"Bear with each other and forgive whatever grievances you may have against one another. Forgive as the Lord forgave you." Colossians 3:13

Key Word

Forgive: To be kind when someone has been mean to you.

Opening Up

Think about a time someone hurt your feelings or was mean to you. What did you want to do? Invite children to respond.

Checking Out God's Word

It's easy to be angry with others who have hurt us. But even when we feel angry, our actions can show forgiveness. When we forgive someone, we can be kind instead of getting revenge. Let's find out why we can forgive instead of staying angry. Read Colossians 3:13 aloud.

■ **Why do you think we should forgive others?**

■ **When has someone forgiven you? Why do you think the person forgave you?**

Jesus told a story about forgiveness in the Bible. Let's read the story to see how Jesus explained forgiveness. Have a child read Matthew 18:21-35 aloud.

■ **What did Peter ask Jesus in verse 21? What was Jesus' response?**

■ **What did the king do to the servant who owed him money?**

■ **What did the servant do to the other servant who owed him money?**

Remembering God's forgiveness and love for us helps us be ready to show love and forgive others. At school, when others are mean and it's hard to forgive, we can ask God's help to forgive others.

Talking to God

Lead children in prayer. **God, You are so kind and loving. Thank You for forgiving our sins. Give us courage to forgive others like You forgave us. In Jesus' name, amen.**

Getting Crafty
Forgiveness Backpack Buddy

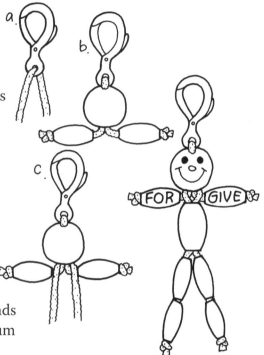

What Each Child Needs

two 12-inch (30.5-cm) pieces of chenille wire

medium-size metal lobster claw

variety of round and oval-shaped wooden beads

scissors

fine-tipped permanent marker

What Each Child Does

1. Thread one end of chenille wire through the small hole at the base of the metal lobster claw (see sketch a). Make sure the chenille wire is equal length. Thread both ends of the chenille wire through a large or medium round-shaped wooden bead for the head.

2. Separate the two pieces of chenille wire and thread one small oval-shaped wooden bead to one piece of the chenille wire. Thread another small oval-shaped wooden bead through the other piece of chenille wire to make arms. Tie knots in both ends of chenille wire to secure the beads (see sketch b). Cut off excess chenille wire.

3. Use second piece of chenille wire to loop around wire in between arms. Make sure the chenille wire is equal length after looping around arms (see sketch c). Thread both ends of the chenille wire through a medium oval-shaped wooden bead to serve as the torso.

4. Separate the two pieces of chenille wire. Thread two small oval-shaped wooden beads (use the same size beads you used for the arms) through one end of chenille wire. Thread two more small oval-shaped wooden beads through the other piece of chenille wire. Tie knots in both ends of chenille wire to secure the beads. Cut off excess chenille wire.

5. Use a fine tipped marker to write "Forgive" across the arms of the Forgiveness Backpack Buddy. Clip the Forgiveness Backpack Buddy to your backpack to remind you to forgive others.

Getting Active

What You Need

masking tape

large paper plates

What You Do

1. **Let's play a game where we think of ways to forgive others.** Divide group into two equal teams. Use masking tape to make two lines approximately 10 feet (3 m) apart. Each team lines up behind one of the lines. Give each team two paper plates. At your signal, the first person on each team stands on the paper plates and moves towards the other group's line by sliding feet on paper plates. After reaching the line, the player picks up the paper plates, runs back to the team and hands the paper plates to the next player in line.

2. When both teams have completed the relay, a volunteer from each team stands together between the two lines. Volunteer from the first team to finish the relay tells a situation in which forgiveness needs to be shown ("someone lied," "broke someone's CD player," "lost a friend's soccer ball"). Volunteer from other team tells a way to either ask for or to give forgiveness in the situation ("offer to pay for something which was broken," "smile and talk to someone to show kindness," "say, 'I'm sorry,'" "promise to tell the truth"). Discuss situations and responses.

3. Repeat the relay as time permits. Vary the relay by challenging children to move sideways or backwards.

Faith Builders at Home

Parents: Use these ideas to help build your child's faith, encouraging your child to become a lifelong follower of Jesus Christ.

"Bear with each other and forgive whatever grievances you may have against one another. Forgive as the Lord forgave you." Colossians 3:13

Key Word

Forgive: To be kind when someone has been mean to you.

Quick Pick

Children love to hear stories about their parents' experiences. Tell your child a story about a time you had to be forgiven or had to forgive someone else.

Fun at Home

Help each other memorize Colossians 3:13 and have some fun at the same time. Print the words of the verse on masking tape with enough space between the words to tear them into separate pieces. One person hides the separate pieces of tape by slightly placing them on objects around the house. Then see how fast other family members can find all the pieces of tape and put them in order.

Steppin' Out

Using colored index cards or construction paper, make "I Forgive You" coupons. Write "I Forgive You" on the card or paper and draw a design to decorate it. Give a coupon to a family member as a way to show forgiveness.

Getting Ready for School

Lesson 38
Patience

"Be completely humble and gentle; be patient, bearing with one another in love."
Ephesians 4:2

Key Word

Patience: To calmly wait for someone or something.

Opening Up

Today we're going to role-play. Let's pretend we're waiting in line to ride a roller coaster at an amusement park. Have children form a single-file line. Ask half of the line to act like people who are waiting patiently. Ask the other half of the line to act like people who are waiting impatiently. After 20 to 30 seconds, have children switch roles. **When are some other times you have to wait?** Invite children to respond.

Checking Out God's Word

When we show patience, we show that we can calmly wait for someone or something. Here's what God's Word says about patience. Read Ephesians 4:2 aloud.

■ **What are some things this verse tells us to be?**

■ **What do you think it means to "bear with one another in love"?**

Showing patience is a great way to show love and kindness. Because God shows His love and kindness to us, we can show love and kindness to others.

Sometimes showing patience to others isn't easy. We can ask God's help to show patience to others when it is hard.

■ **How has someone shown patience to you?**

■ **When might it be hard for a kid your age to show patience to others? When might it be easy?**

Talking to God

Have children form pairs. (Optional: Have children form pairs according to height similarity.) Have children tell each other one way he or she will show patience to someone else this week. **Let's thank God for the patience He shows us and ask for His help in showing patience to others.** Lead children in prayer. **Father God, thank You for the patience You show us. Help us to show patience to others. In Jesus' name, amen.**

Getting Crafty
Patience Pencil Holders

What Each Child Needs

scissors

card stock

marker

cardboard cylinder about 5 inches
   (12.5 cm) tall

glue

yarn in a variety of colors

paint or glue brush

What Each Child Does

1. Cut a 2-inch (5-cm) strip of card stock long enough to fit around the rim of the cylinder. Use a marker to write "Have Patience" on the strip of paper.

2. Glue the strip of paper around the top of the cylinder so the writing can be seen. Brush a thin layer of glue over the unglued sides of the container.

3. Wrap the yarn around the sides of the container, beginning at the bottom of the container. To change yarn colors, cut the yarn and begin wrapping a new color of yarn where you stopped wrapping the previous color.

4. Continue process until you have wrapped yarn up to the bottom of the paper.

5. Keep this pencil holder nearby when you do your homework. You'll not only have pencils and pens handy, but it will be a reminder to be patient.

Getting Active

What You Need

masking tape or chalk

What You Do

1. **God wants us to show patience in everything we do. Let's play a game of tag where we need to show patience.** Make two parallel masking-tape lines at least 15 to 25 feet (4.5 m to 8 m) apart and at least 10 feet (3 m) long. (Use chalk if you are playing on asphalt.)

2. Choose one child to be "It." "It" stands between the two lines. All other children stand behind one line.

3. At your signal, children run past "It" and across the opposite line, trying not to be tagged by "It." If a child is tagged, that child freezes in place and begins touching his or her head, shoulders, knees and then toes, repeating movements over and over again.

4. At your signal, children who successfully crossed run back to the opposite line, tagging any frozen children to unfreeze them. Any new children who are tagged by "It" must freeze in place and repeat the motions until they are freed by another child.

5. Continue giving signal for children to run back and forth between the masking-tape lines. Every few minutes, substitute a new volunteer to be "It." Continue game as time allows.

Faith Builders at Home

Parents: Use these ideas to help build your child's faith, encouraging your child to become a lifelong follower of Jesus Christ.

> "Be completely humble and gentle; be patient, bearing with one another in love."
> Ephesians 4:2
>
> ## Key Word
>
> **Patience: To calmly wait for someone or something.**

Steppin' Out

On your next visit to the grocery store together, model patience for your children by letting someone in front of you in line during the register check-out.

Fun at Home

Play a game like "Pictionary." Take turns drawing ways to show patience to others. See how fast you can guess the patient actions.

Quick Pick

Invent a hand signal to give when someone wants something but needs to wait (a thumbs up, sign language for the letter P—closed fist with pointer and middle finger pointed down, etc.). Plan to use the signal when you need someone to wait for you, or as a signal to show that you are waiting for someone else!

God's Protection

Lesson 39
Strong and Courageous

"Be strong and courageous. Do not be terrified; do not be discouraged, for the Lord your God will be with you wherever you go." Joshua 1:9

Key Word

Courage: To be brave when you are facing danger or difficulty.

Opening Up

What are some things you think kids younger than you might be afraid of? Older than you? The same age as you? Invite children to tell ideas.

Checking Out God's Word

Everyone is afraid sometimes. Being afraid can be a good thing if it keeps us from doing something dangerous. But when we do feel afraid, listen to what the Bible says the followers of Jesus can remember. Have a child read Joshua 1:9 aloud. When we're afraid, the Bible tells us to have courage. Having courage means to be brave when we have something hard to do or we are in a difficult situation.

■ How would you say Joshua 1:9 in your own words?

■ What do you know about God that helps you depend on Him?

No matter what the situation may be, God promises to be with us wherever we go! He will give us courage and help us know what to do, even when we're afraid.

■ Where do kids your age go? When might they need courage in those places?

Talking to God

Lead children in prayer, thanking God for always being with them and for helping us have courage. (Optional: Help children form pairs. Tell your partner a situation in which you want to show courage. Pray with your partner and ask God to help him or her be strong and courageous. Thank God for always being with your partner, no matter where he or she may go.)

Getting Crafty
Courage Necklace

What Each Child Needs

plastic letter beads

thin plastic cord

scissors

plastic pony beads in various colors

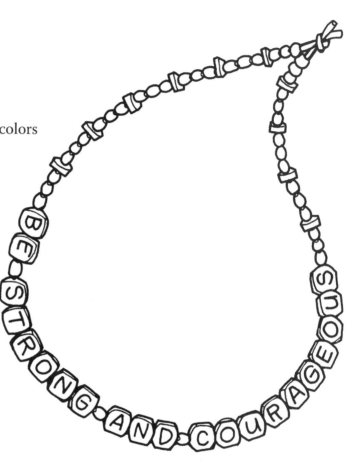

What Each Child Does

1. Sort through the letter beads to find all the letters for "BE STRONG AND COURAGEOUS." Lay the beads out in word order. Cut a 24-inch (61 cm) length of plastic cord.

2. To start the necklace, tie the cord around one pony bead in a knot so the beads won't slip off. Begin stringing the beads as desired. (Optional: Form a pattern with different colored beads.) Use a colored bead as a spacer between each word.

3. Tie the end of the necklace to the first bead securely. (Optional: Wear necklaces as a reminder of how to have courage.)

Getting Active

What You Need

Bible

index cards

marker

cardboard box

pushpins

What You Do

1. Print Joshua 1:9 on index cards, one word or short phrase on each card. Prepare at least one card for each child. Place box, pushpins, and a set of ordered verse cards on one side of the playing area.

2. Children line up on one side of the playing area, opposite from box.

3. At your signal, the first child in line runs to the box, takes the top verse card, attaches card to box with pushpin and returns to his team. Next child in line repeats action. Children attempt to attach verse cards in order to box. Continue until all cards are attached to box. Read verse aloud. Repeat relay as time permits, mixing up the order of the verse cards so that children must put them in order as they complete the relay.

Faith Builders at Home

Parents: Use these ideas to help build your child's faith, encouraging your child to become a lifelong follower of Jesus Christ.

"Be strong and courageous. Do not be terrified; do not be discouraged, for the Lord your God will be with you wherever you go." Joshua 1:9

Key Word

Courage: To be brave when you are facing danger or difficulty.

Fun at Home

Give each family member a sheet of paper and pen. Each person writes his or her own paraphrase of Joshua 1:9 on the paper. Put the papers where you can see them every day. (Optional: In a notebook, work together to write a family paraphrase of the verse. Each week choose a different verse to paraphrase and write it in your notebook.).

Quick Pick

On a Christian music CD, find a song that talks about the help God offers us in difficult situations. At bedtime or in the car, listen to the song together. At the end of the song, thank God for the courage He gives us.

Steppin' Out

Ask a grandparent, your child's Sunday School teacher, small group leader, or a pastor at your church to tell your family about a time God helped them when they needed courage in a difficult time.

God's Protection

Lesson 40
Truth and Righteousness

"Be strong in the Lord and in his mighty power. Put on the full armor of God."
Ephesians 6:10-11

Key Word

Righteousness: To think and do what God says is right.

Opening Up

If you were in a battle, what kind of protection would you want to have? What kinds of things would you do to prepare for a battle? Invite children to tell ideas.

Checking Out God's Word

The Bible tells us that when we obey and follow God it's like being a soldier. Read Ephesians 6:10-11 aloud. **God gives us protection just like a soldier wears armor to be protected in a battle.**

- Read Ephesians 6:14. **A belt wraps all the way around your waist. What does this verse say our belt is? Why do you think it's so important to know what is true about God?**

- Another word for "breastplate" is "body armor." What does verse 14 say our body armor is? To be righteous means to think and do what is right. How do you learn what is right?

The protection God gives us is sometimes called the armor of God. Read Ephesians 6:10-11 aloud again. **When we wear this armor we can stand up for God's commands and obey Him, rather than obeying God's enemy, the devil. It's good to know we can depend on God's protection no matter where we are or what happens to us.**

Talking to God

Let's pray and thank God for the protection He gives us. Lead children in prayer. Thank God for helping us learn what is true about Him, and ask His help in thinking and doing what is right.

Getting Crafty
Belt and Breastplate

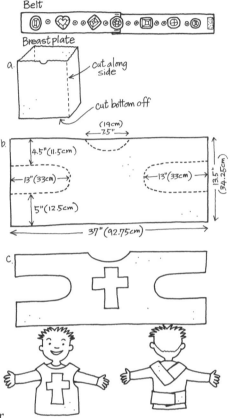

What Each Child Needs

2 3x18-inch (7.5x45.5-cm) strips of
   brown craft foam

stapler

4 sets of adhesive Velcro dots

plastic jewels

markers

craft glue

scissors

large brown grocery bag

silver paint

gold paint

sponge paintbrush

What Each Child Does

Part 1: Belt

1. Staple the brown craft foam strips together
   at one end. Measure it around your waist, leaving enough room for the ends to
   overlap two inches. Cut off the extra craft foam.

2. Stick two Velcro dots to the ends of the craft foam so that the opposite ends connect when the belt is wrapped around your waist. If needed, staple the Velcro dots
   to secure them.

3. Glue plastic jewels onto the belt. Make sure that you are decorating the side of the
   belt that faces outward. Set aside to dry before wearing.

Part 2: Breastplate

1. Cut a large brown paper bag as shown in sketches a and b.

2. Paint one side of the bag with silver paint. Paint a large gold cross in the center of
   the bag as shown in sketch c. Let the paint dry completely before moving on to
   the next step.

3. Criss-cross the straps from the bag around your back. Use Velcro dots to secure
   them in place. If needed, staple dots in place.

Getting Active

What You Need

index cards

marker

children's music CD and player

stopwatch or clock with second hand

What You Do

1. Print each letter of the word "righteousness" and "truth" on separate index cards and mix them together with enough other blank index cards to provide one card for each child.

2. Children sit or stand in a circle. Give each child an index card facedown.

3. As you play music, children pass cards facedown around the circle. Stop the music after a short while. When the music stops, children look at their cards. Children with blank cards do five jumping jacks. Children with letters on their cards move quickly to stand in correct order to spell "righteousness" or "truth." Use a stopwatch or clock with a second hand to time how fast children can spell words correctly.

4. Collect index cards, mix cards together and redistribute to play again. Continue game as time as allows, changing the actions of children holding blank cards (high-five a friend, turn around twice, etc.).

Faith Builders at Home

Parents: Use these ideas to help build your child's faith, encouraging your child to become a lifelong follower of Jesus Christ.

"Be strong in the Lord and in his mighty power. Put on the full armor of God."
Ephesians 6:10-11

Key Word

Righteousness: To think and do what God says is right.

Steppin' Out

Just for fun, build up some arm strength by arm wrestling with someone in your family. Then build up some strength in being righteous by reading these Bible commands and telling a way to obey each one: Matthew 5:44; Romans 15:1-2; Ephesians 4:1-2.

Quick Pick

Ask each person in your family to find and read one of these Bible passages: Psalm 23; Psalm 121; Isaiah 40:28-31. Talk about this question: What do you learn about God's protection from these verses?

Fun at Home

Read Ephesians 6:10-11 together. Then work together to create motions to represent each phrase of the verse. When you've thought of motions for the entire verse, repeat the verse with motions several times. Then one person does the motions for any phrase in the verse. Other family members say the phrase. Repeat procedure several times until each family member has had a turn to choose phrase.

God's Protection

Lesson 41
Salvation and Peace

"Salvation comes from the Lord."
Jonah 2:9

Key Word

Salvation: To be rescued from sin.

Opening Up

If you could a design a hat, what would it look like? What if you could design a pair of shoes, what would they look like? Invite children to tell ideas.

Checking Out God's Word

The Bible tells us about some special things that God gives the members of His family to protect them and keep them safe. The Bible uses the parts of a soldier's uniform to describe these ways that God protects us. Let's read about the kind of helmet and shoes God has designed for us to wear.

■ Read Ephesians 6:17 aloud. **What does this verse say that salvation is like? Why is having a strong helmet so important?**

When we are saved, we are protected from the consequences of sin. Jesus died on the cross so that we can be forgiven for all our sins. The Bible says in Jonah 2:9 that salvation comes from the Lord.

■ Read Ephesians 6:15 aloud. **What does this verse say that we need to have on our feet? How does wearing shoes protect us every day?**

When we wear shoes, we are protecting our feet from getting bruised and hurt. We're ready to walk and run fast! In the same way, God wants us to be quick to tell others about the peace and salvation He offers to each person.

Talking to God

Let's pray to God and thank Him for His helmet of salvation and shoes of peace. Lead children in prayer. **Thank You God for protecting us from sin by giving us salvation. Help us to be ready to tell others about the peace You give. In Jesus' name, amen.**

Getting Crafty
Helmet and Shoes

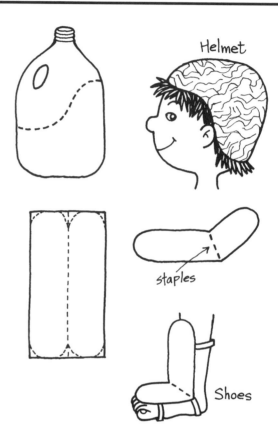

Helmet

staples

Shoes

What Each Child Needs

clean, empty gallon milk jug

scissors

aluminum foil

transparent tape

1 large sheet of black or brown
   craft foam

6¹/₄ x 8-inch (.6x20.5-cm)
   elastic strips

stapler

What Each Child Does

Part 1: Helmet of Salvation

1. Have an adult cut handle off the milk jug and help you trim jug until it fits on your head.

2. Cover entire helmet with aluminum foil. Use transparent tape to secure aluminum foil to helmet.

Part 2: Shoes of Peace

1. Cut large sheet of black or brown craft foam in half lengthwise. On each sheet, cut the ends to round the corners.

2. Fold each piece of craft foam over about one third of the way and staple it three or four times across the fold.

3. The smaller section of craft foam should lay flat on your foot. The larger section of craft foam should extend up the leg. The staples should be facing inward. Staple three elastic straps to each shoe. One strap should be near the top, one near the ankle, and one under the ball of the foot.

Getting Active

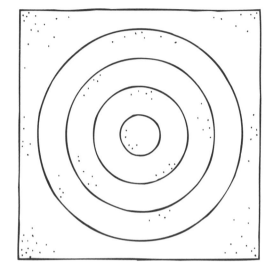

What You Need

large sheets of paper

markers

masking tape

index cards

scissors

one blindfold for every eight children

What You Do

1. Draw several circles inside of each other on a large sheet of paper (see sketch), making one paper target for every eight children. Tape target(s) onto wall at eye level of children. Cut index cards in half.

2. Give each child half of an index card. Child draws a large X on the card and writes initials in one corner. Children make masking-tape loops to put on the backs of their cards.

3. Play a game similar to Pin the Tail on the Donkey. Children stand in single-file lines of no more than eight children each, approximately 5 feet (1.5 m) away from a target. Blindfold the first children in each line. Each blindfolded child walks to the target and tries to stick his or her X on the center of the target. Then child takes off blindfold and returns to the end of the line. Next child in line is blindfolded and takes a turn. Repeat activity until all children have had a turn. Child whose X is closest to the center of the target tells a way that God gives protection to or helps the members of His family (answers prayer, forgives sin, gives courage, etc.).

Faith Builders at Home

Parents: Use these ideas to help build your child's faith, encouraging your child to become a lifelong follower of Jesus Christ.

"Salvation comes from the Lord."
Jonah 2:9

Key Word

Salvation: To be rescued from sin.

Quick Pick

Write these questions on separate index cards or slips of paper: Who first told you about Jesus? How did you learn about God's plan of salvation? What happened when you decided to become a Christian? What's the best part about being a child of God? Put the questions in a bowl or hat. Let your child take turns choosing cards or papers and reading the questions aloud to interview Mom or Dad or older siblings.

Fun at Home

Make a reminder of the salvation God gives us by using rainbow writing. You'll need paper and three colors of one of these materials: crayons, markers, yarn, ribbon or glitter pens. Print the word "salvation" with one color of the material you want to use. Outline the letters with the second color, and then the third color. Display the completed reminder in your kitchen or family room.

Steppin' Out

Help your family think about the variety of people to whom we can be ready to share the gospel of peace. Look through magazines together to find and cut out pictures of as many different kinds of people as possible—age, nationality, physical characteristics, etc. See how many pictures your family can find. Glue the pictures to a large piece of paper.

God's Protection

Lesson 42
Faith and the Word of God

"In addition to all this, take up the shield of faith, with which you can extinguish all the flaming arrows of the evil one." Ephesians 6:16

Key Word

Faith: To be certain about the things we cannot see.

Opening Up

Collect a blindfold and ask for two volunteers. Have one volunteer put on a blindfold. **We're going to take a short walk around the room. Your partner without the blindfold will lead you.** Allow a few moments for children to walk around the room. Then have children switch roles. **How did it feel to trust your partner to lead you around the room? Was it hard or easy to trust someone when you could not see? Why?** (Optional: As time permits, allow more than one pair of children to participate.)

Checking Out God's Word

Trusting someone else can be hard. When we are part of God's family, however, we know that we can always trust God. God protects us by giving us a shield. Let's find out what the shield is. Choose a child to read Ephesians 6:16 aloud.

■ **What do soldiers use shields for?**

■ **What does this verse say our shield is? What does this shield protect us from?**

"The evil one" is a name for God's enemy, the devil. God's enemy does not want us to believe in God or to show how much we love and obey God. When we depend on God and have faith in Him, it's like we have a shield to keep us safe. The Bible tells us about something we can use to protect ourselves from God's enemy, the devil. Choose a child to read Ephesians 6:17 aloud.

■ **What does this verse say is like a sword?**

The Bible, or Word of God, protects us from God's enemy. When we know and obey God's Word, we show God's enemy that we believe and trust only in God's power.

Talking to God

Let's pray and thank God for the ways He protects us as we have faith in Him and read His Word. Lead children in prayer.

Getting Crafty
Sword and Shield

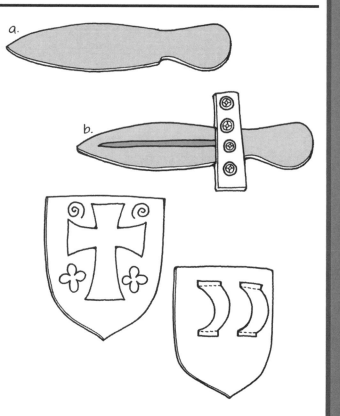

What Each Child Needs

13x18-inch (33x45.5-cm) sheet of
black craft foam

scissors

craft glue

pencil

silver paint

thin paintbrush

2 sheets of 8.5x11-inch (21.5x28-cm)
colored craft foam (any color)

plastic jewels

half sheet of poster board

markers

packing tape

What Each Child Does

Part 1: Sword of the Spirit

1. Cut black craft foam in half length-wise. Glue pieces together for double thickness.

2. Draw the shape of a sword on the black craft foam as shown in sketch a. Cut sword shape through both pieces of black craft foam.

3. Make a thin stripe down the center of the sword blade with silver paint as shown in sketch b.

4. Draw the shape of a sword handle on one sheet of colored craft foam. Place the other sheet of colored craft foam on the bottom of the first sheet. Cut the shape of the sword handle to make two handles. Glue handles onto sides of the sword as shown in sketch b. Glue plastic jewels on the sword handle.

Part 2: Shield of Faith

1. Cut a 2-inch (5-cm) strip from the short side of poster board. Cut the strip in half. Set aside to use later.

2. Draw the shape of a shield on the poster board and cut out. Use markers to decorate.

3. Turn over shield. Use two strips of poster board as handles on back of shield. Tape the handles to the back of shield.

Getting Active

What You Need

Bible
Post-it Notes
marker
10 empty plastic water bottles
paper
pencils
tennis ball

What You Do

1. Print the words and reference of Ephesians 6:16 on Post-it Notes, one word on each note. Stick each note on a plastic bottle. Also print words and reference of Ephesians 6:16 on a sheet of paper. Photocopy one paper for each child. Set plastic bottles in a bowling-pin formation on one side of the playing area.

2. Give each child a verse paper and a pencil. Ask a child to read the verse aloud. Children line up about 7 feet (2.1 m) from the verse bottles.

3. The first child in line rolls the tennis ball at the bottles. Child takes verse paper and pencil over to bottles and reads words on the knocked-over bottles. Child crosses off those words on the verse paper, returns bottles to original positions and goes to the end of the line. Next child in line repeats action. Play continues until all children have crossed off all words on their papers. The children who finish first may assist the other children by reading words on bottles and setting them back in place.

Faith Builders at Home

Parents: Use these ideas to help build your child's faith, encouraging your child to become a lifelong follower of Jesus Christ.

"In addition to all this, take up the shield of faith, with which you can extinguish all the flaming arrows of the evil one." Ephesians 6:16

Key Word

Faith: To be certain about the things we cannot see.

Steppin' Out

Collect a set of building blocks or toys (Legos, cardboard blocks, etc). Build a tower together with each family member adding a block or toy one at a time. As each block is added, family member completes the sentence, "I can show faith in God by loving and obeying Him when I. . . ."

Fun at Home

Cover a tabletop or counter with a large sheet of paper. Use a marker or crayon and draw lines to divide the paper into three sections. At the top of each section, write "School," "Church," and "Home." Give each family member a marker or crayon. Have each family member write in designated sections one way to show faith in God at school, church and home. Discuss what was written at a mealtime or right before bedtime.

Quick Pick

Look at Hebrews 11:4-31 for examples of people who showed their faith in God. Choose one of the people and read his or her story in the Bible.

Hanging Out with God

Lesson 43
Worship

> "Therefore, I urge you, brothers, in view of God's mercy, to offer your bodies as living sacrifices, holy and pleasing to God—this is your spiritual act of worship."
> Romans 12:1

Key Word

Worship: To show love and respect.

Opening Up

Help children form pairs. **With your partner, think of a definition for the word "worship."** Have pairs share their responses with the group.

Checking Out God's Word

Some people may think that worshiping God means to sing songs or to pray. Praying and singing songs to God are good things to do. But worship means more than singing songs or praying. In Romans 12:1 the Bible tells us about worship. Have a child read Romans 12:1 aloud.

■ **This verse talks about God's mercy. What has God done for us that we don't deserve?**

Because of God's great love and forgiveness for us, Romans 12:1 says we can offer our bodies to God. When we offer our bodies to God as living sacrifices, it means we live so that everything we do shows God how much we love Him. It's how we worship God. Worship is showing love and respect to God every day no matter where we are.

■ **What is a way to show God how much you love and respect Him when you're at school? At home with your family?**

■ **What can you do to worship God when you're doing chores? Doing your homework? Playing with your friends?**

Every time we obey one of God's commands or do our best at school or on a sports team, we are living in a way that shows God how much we love and respect Him.

Talking to God

Give each child a slip of paper and a pencil. Have each child write his or her name on the paper. Put papers in a basket or container. Have each child choose a name from the basket and then find the child whose name is on the paper. **Tell your partner one way you will worship God today.** Allow time for children to respond. Then lead children in prayer. **Thank You, God, for showing us how to worship You. Help us to show love and respect to You every day. In Jesus' name, amen.**

Getting Crafty
God's Gift

What Each Child Needs

shoe box or other small box

scissors

3x5-inch (7.5x12.5-cm) photo of him- or herself

wrapping paper

tape

construction paper

ribbon or bow

optional—3x5-inch (7.5x12.5-cm) paper or index card, markers

What Each Child Does

1. Remove the lid from box and carefully cut a small rectangle in one end of the box. Fold the bottom of your picture over 1/2 inch (1.3 cm). Tape picture inside box facing the rectangle opening. (Optional: If photo is not available, child draws a picture of self on paper or index card.)

2. Replace the lid on box. Wrap entire box, except the opening, with wrapping paper. Make sure not to wrap opening so you can look inside and see your picture. Add a ribbon or bow on top of box.

3. Draw a gift tag on a sheet of construction paper. Cut out the gift tag. Write "To: God, From: (Justin)" and add your name. Tape gift tag on box lid.

Getting Active

What You Need

large sheet of paper

marker

tape

What You Do

1. Print Romans 12:1 on a large sheet of paper and display paper where children can read it.

2. Ask a child to read Romans 12:1 aloud. Children stand in a circle. In order around the circle, assign each child a word from the verse for which to create a motion. Each child thinks of and practices a simple motion for his or her word.

3. To begin, the child with the first word of the verse says the word while doing motion. The next child says the first word while doing the first child's motion and then says his or her own word while doing his or her own motion. Continue around the circle, each child saying and doing the previous words and motions and adding his or her own word and motion until the entire verse is recited with motions. Invite children to try saying the entire verse with motions.

Faith Builders at Home

Parents: Use these ideas to help build your child's faith, encouraging your child to become a lifelong follower of Jesus Christ.

"Therefore, I urge you, brothers, in view of God's mercy, to offer your bodies as living sacrifices, holy and pleasing to God—this is your spiritual act of worship."
Romans 12:1

Key Word

Worship: To show love and respect.

Quick Pick

On a white board or sheet of paper, list the days of the week. For each day, decide with your family a way you will all worship God (be kind, pray together, help someone, etc.). Display the board or paper where everyone will see it. At the end of each day, each person who remembered to worship God in the listed way, writes his or her initials by the day of the week.

Fun at Home

Play a game of Concentration. On a sheet of paper draw a grid with equal numbers of rows and columns, making at least 12 squares the size of large Post-it Notes. In each square, write a way to worship God, writing each way to worship God two times. Cover each square with a large Post-it Note. (Optional: Cut pieces of paper and lightly tape them over each square.) Family members take turns lifting up two Post-it Notes at a time to match the ways to worship God.

Steppin' Out

When you're outside at a park or taking a walk, or driving in the car (take a different route just for fun), take turns "spying" things for which you can worship God (something God created, a person you can help or who helps you, etc.). See who can spy the most things!

Hanging Out with God

Lesson 44
Celebrating Who God Is

"Let everything that has breath praise the Lord. Praise the Lord." Psalm 150:6

Key Word

**Praise: To celebrate and tell someone the things
we love about him or her.**

Opening Up

**What does it mean to praise someone?
Who has praised you? What did you
receive praise for?** Invite children to
respond.

Checking Out God's Word

**Just like we can receive or give praise
to someone else, we can praise God.
Psalm 150 tells us about praising God.**
Have a child read Psalm 150 aloud.

■ **What are some reasons Psalm 150
says we can praise God?**

■ **What are some of the different ways
we can praise God?**

**We can praise God by singing songs,
playing music, writing poems, drawing
pictures, or just shouting it out! When
we praise God, we are celebrating and
telling Him the things we love about
Him.**

■ **What's your favorite way to praise
God?**

■ **What might happen when other
people hear our praise to God?**

Talking to God

**Today we're going to praise God
together by telling ways to finish this
sentence, "God, You are so. . . ."** Allow
a few minutes for children to think of
ways to finish the sentence. Then begin
the prayer by saying, **Dear God, You
deserve all of our praise. You do
great things for us. You are so. . . .**
Volunteers tell ideas for finishing the
sentence. (Optional: Write sentences
on paper.) End the prayer time by
saying, **God, we love You. In Jesus'
name, amen.**

Getting Crafty
Praise Drum

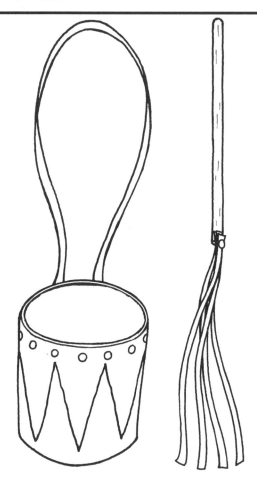

What Each Child Needs

newspaper

paper plate

acrylic or tempera paint (any color)

empty oatmeal container

scissors

acrylic or tempera paintbrush

12-inch (30.5-cm) wooden dowel

8 ft. (2.4 m) length of ribbon

thumbtack

hole punch

What Each Child Does

1. Lay newspaper over your workspace. Pour a small amount of paint onto the paper plate.

2. With an adult's help, cut the oatmeal container in half. Set aside the top half of container.

3. Paint the bottom half of oatmeal container and the wooden dowel and let dry.

4. Cut ribbon into four or five 12-inch (30.5-cm) pieces. Carefully push the thumbtack through one end of each ribbon. Push the thumbtack with ribbons firmly into one end of wooden dowel.

5. Punch two holes in the oatmeal container, about 1-inch (2.5-cm) apart. Thread a 36-inch (91.5-cm) piece of ribbon through the holes and tie ends together to create a loop to fit over your head.

6. Use your drum to play along with a song of praise to God.

Getting Active

What You Need

3-inch (7.5-cm) construction paper squares (at least 10 squares for each child)

markers

stopwatch or watch with a second hand

What You Do

1. Give each child 10 squares of paper and a marker. Children number squares 1 to 10 and then randomly place squares on floor, numbered side down, spreading out squares as much as possible throughout the playing area.

2. Divide group into teams. Teams line up shoulder-to-shoulder on opposite sides of the playing area. Assign numbers to children as in the game Steal the Bacon (see sketch).

3. Call two numbers. Children with those numbers from each team have five seconds to collect as many construction-paper squares as possible. Call "Stop" when time is up; children return to teams with the squares they collected and add the numbers on the squares. Volunteer(s) from the team with the highest number total tells a reason to praise God.

4. To play another round, volunteers return squares to playing area, numbered side down. Play as many rounds at time allows. (Replaced crumpled squares as needed.)

Faith Builders at Home

Parents: Use these ideas to help build your child's faith, encouraging your child to become a lifelong follower of Jesus Christ.

"Let everything that has breath praise the Lord. Praise the Lord." Psalm 150:6

Key Word

Praise: To celebrate and tell someone the things we love about him or her.

Fun at Home

Designate one night this week as Praise Night. On a large sheet of paper, write the words of Psalm 150:6. Draw pictures and symbols that illustrate the words. Then each family member writes a sentence prayer of praise to God. Display the paper as a reminder to praise God.

Quick Pick

For each letter of the alphabet, see if your family can write down something that begins with that letter for which you can praise God.

Steppin' Out

Give each family member one minute to find a household item or two that can be used as a rhythm instrument (two spoons to tap together, shake a box of pasta, tap the bottom of a pan, etc.). Experiment with the instruments and then play them while listening to song of praise to God on a CD.

 The Big Book of Bible Lessons for Crafty Kids

Hanging Out with God

Lesson 45
Answers to Prayer

"Therefore I tell you, whatever you ask for in prayer, believe that you have received it, and it will be yours." Mark 11:24

Key Word

Prayer: To talk and listen to God.

Opening Up

When was the last time that you asked someone for help? Did you receive the help you asked for? Why or why not? Invite children to respond.

Checking Out God's Word

Sometimes when we can't do things ourselves, we have to ask for help. Today we're going to talk about asking God for help. The Bible tells us a story of a church that prayed and asked God for His help. Read Acts 12:1-16 aloud. (Optional: Have the child whose birthday is closest to today to read.)

■ **Why do you think Peter was put in prison?**

■ **What do you think the church was praying for?**

■ **How did God answer the prayers of the people of the church? Why were they surprised when they saw Peter?**

■ **When was a time that God has answered your prayer? Were you surprised?**

Prayer is a way for us to talk and listen to God. Here's what God promises us. Read Mark 11:24 aloud. **God always listens to our prayers, and He promises to answer our prayers in a way that is best for us. He may answer by saying "yes" or "no" or He may answer by giving us something better than what we asked for!**

Talking to God

Have children tell three people one way they need God's help this week. Then lead children in prayer, inviting each child to pray silently for the requests they were told. End the prayer time by saying, **Dear God, thank You so much for listening to us when we pray and for promising to answer our prayers for help. In Jesus' name, amen.** (Optional: Before leading them in prayer, have children complete prayer journal as instructed on next page. Children use journal to record prayer requests.)

Getting Crafty
Patchwork Prayer Journal

What Each Child Needs

composition book or other
  paper notebook
glue stick
several patterns of wrapping
  paper cut into 1- to 2-inch
  (2.5- to 5-cm) squares
scissors
construction paper
markers or crayons
optional—fabric squares instead
  of paper squares

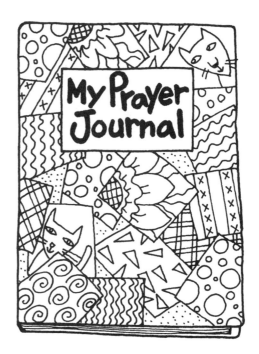

What Each Child Does

1. Spread glue on the back of a wrapping paper square. (Optional: Use fabric square.) Place square onto the front or back cover of composition book. Smooth out paper.

2. Repeat process, overlapping edges of paper until entire front and back of the composition book are covered.

3. On a 2x5-inch (5x12.5-cm) piece of construction paper, write "My Prayer Journal." Glue paper into place on the front cover of book. Allow time to dry. Write or draw your prayer requests or the prayer requests of your family in your journal.

Getting Active

What You Need

sheet of paper

markers

Post-it Notes

optional—masking tape

What You Do

1. Print the sentence "God answers my prayer" on the sheet of paper.

2. Give each child a Post-it Note. Assign each child a word from the sentence "God answers my prayer," repeating words as needed. Children write assigned words on their Post-it Notes, referring as necessary to paper you prepared. Each child puts his or her Post-it Note on his or her back, legs, arms or feet. (Optional: Use masking tape to attach notes securely.)

3. Children begin moving around the playing area. At your signal, children find others with different words from the sentence and line up in order to spell out sentence. Group of children who form sentence first are the winners.

4. Repeat game as time permits. Vary the game by inviting students to suggest other information they know about prayer with which to play the game ("I can pray every day." "God listens to me.")

Faith Builders at Home

Parents: Use these ideas to help build your child's faith, encouraging your child to become a lifelong follower of Jesus Christ.

"Therefore I tell you, whatever you ask for in prayer, believe that you have received it, and it will be yours." Mark 11:24

Key Word

Prayer: To talk and listen to God.

Fun at Home

Buy finger paints or glitter pens. Use finger paints or glitter pens to write a prayer on paper. Hang your painted prayers on your child's bedroom wall or on a refrigerator as a reminder to pray every day.

Quick Pick

When involved in a favorite activity with your child, look for an opportunity to pray a short, simple prayer related to the activity. For example, thank God for your child's abilities in playing a game or putting together a puzzle.

Steppin' Out

Sometimes children find it difficult to know what to say to God. At bedtime or mealtime, ask a question or two to motivate their prayers: What is something you want to thank God for? What is something you are glad happened today? What is something you want to ask God's help with?

Hanging Out with God

Lesson 46
Giving Thanks (Thanksgiving)

> "Give thanks in all circumstances, for this is God's will for you in Christ Jesus."
> 1 Thessalonians 5:18

Key Word

Thanks: To tell someone how much you appreciate him or her.

Opening Up

What is something really good that might happen to a kid your age? What would make you say that you are having a really good day? Invite children to tell ideas.

Checking Out God's Word

It's fun to think about the good things that we like to have happen to us, and it's easy to thank God for those good things. But sometimes we have days that aren't so good. Some days we might feel like nothing good is happening to us. The Bible says in 1 Thessalonians 5:18 that we can give thanks in all circumstances. This means that no matter what situation we may be facing, we can always be grateful to God. Let's read about a story about two men who thanked God—even on a pretty bad day! Have a child read Acts 16:16-31 aloud. (Optional: Have a child closest to age ten read aloud.)

■ What made Paul and Silas sing praise to God? What do you think they praised Him for?

■ How did God show that He was with Paul and Silas?

■ What do you know about God that you can thank Him for—even on a bad day?

We might not always feel like we want to thank and praise God. But thanking Him reminds us that He does love us and will help us in every circumstance—good or bad!

Talking to God

Let's thank God today by using "popcorn prayers." After I start the prayer, anyone can take a turn to pray by saying the name of something you're thankful for. Our prayers can pop as quickly as popcorn! Begin the prayer time by saying, "Thank You God for. . . ." Volunteers say names of things for which they are thankful. End the prayer time by thanking God for always being with us and loving us in good or bad times.

Getting Crafty
Thanksgiving Tree

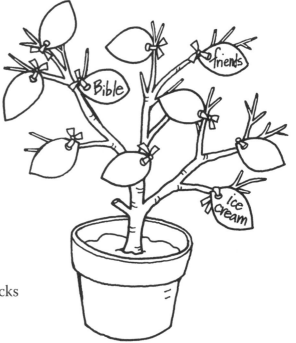

What Each Child Needs

small clay pot

packing tape

plaster of paris

mixing bowl

water

small tree branch with leaves removed

markers or pens

green construction paper

green ribbon

scissors

hole punch

optional—16 ounce plastic cup, small rocks
   and dirt, paint and paintbrushes

What Each Child Does

1. Place a piece of packing tape on the inside bottom of the pot to cover any hole(s).
   (Optional: Instead of a clay pot, use a 16 ounce plastic cup.) With an adult's help,
   mix plaster of paris with water, according to directions on package to fill the pot
   3/4 full. (Optional: Instead of plaster of paris, use small rocks and dirt to prop up
   your branch.)

2. Have an adult help you pour plaster into clay pot and let sit for one or two minutes until slightly firm. Push the branch into center of pot. The branch should be
   able to stand on its own. If not, let the plaster dry for a few more minutes. Once
   the branch is standing, set pot aside.

3. Draw and cut 10 (or desired amount) leaf shapes from green construction paper.
   Punch a hole into one end of each leaf.

4. On several leaves, write things that you are thankful for. Keep extra leaves handy
   so that you may add to your tree as you think of more things to thank God for.)
   Then tie leaves to the branch with green ribbon to create a Thanksgiving tree.
   (Optional: For an added splash of color, paint your pot with craft paints.)

Getting Active

What You Need

empty soda can for each child

children's music CD and player

optional—colored index cards

What You Do

1. Play a game like Musical Chairs with children. Children form a large circle, standing about 1 foot (30.5 cm) apart. Give each child a soda can to place at his or her feet. (Optional: Substitute colored index cards for soda cans.) Ask one volunteer to put his or her can to the side of the playing area, away from the circle.

2. Start the music. Children begin to walk clockwise around the cans. When you stop the music, each child picks up the closest can. The child left without a can tells one thing he or she is thankful to God for.

Faith Builders at Home

Parents: Use these ideas to help build your child's faith, encouraging your child to become a lifelong follower of Jesus Christ.

"Give thanks in all circumstances, for this is God's will for you in Christ Jesus."
1 Thessalonians 5:18

Key Word

Thanks: To tell someone how much you appreciate him or her.

Steppin' Out

Buy a tally counter at an office supply store (or keep a pad of Post-it Notes and pen handy). For one whole day while you are with your child at home, at the grocery store, at church, in the car or visiting friends, count how many times he or she says "thank you" to others. When you hear him or her say "thank you," click your counter (or put a tally mark on a Post-it Note). At the end of the day, show your child the number of times he or she said "thank you." Then enjoy a celebration thank-you snack together.

Quick Pick

Give each family member a piece of aluminum foil. Without using scissors, give each person five minutes to create something they are thankful to God for with the foil. Display foil creations on a mantle or bookcase as a reminder to give thanks to God.

Fun at Home

Visit the Internet and search for different ways to say "thank you" in other languages. During a prayer time in your home, end or start a prayer by saying "thank you" to God in another language.

Hanging Out with God

Lesson 47
Listening to God

"Then Samuel said, 'Speak, for your servant is listening.'"
1 Samuel 3:10

Key Word

Listen: To pay attention to what someone says.

Opening Up

Who is your best friend? How would your friendship be different if you never listened to what each other said? Invite children to respond.

Checking Out God's Word

When we listen to someone else, it means that we are paying attention to what the person says. Just like we can listen to our friends when they speak, we can listen when God is speaking to us, too. The Bible tells us a story about a boy named Samuel who listened to God. Have a child read 1 Samuel 3:1-11 aloud.

■ Why did Samuel keep going to Eli? How do you think Samuel felt when Eli kept sending him back to bed?

■ What did Eli finally tell Samuel to do?

■ What are some ways that God speaks to us today? (Through the Bible. Through other Christians. Through prayer.)

We can listen to God every day. When we read God's Word or talk to another Christian, we can pay attention to the things God wants us to do. When we pray, we can be quiet and wait for God's Holy Spirit to help us know right things to do.

Talking to God

Let's pray and talk to God right now. In part of our prayer time, we'll talk to God silently and then be quiet to listen to Him. Lead children in a prayer time. Begin by saying, **Dear God, we're glad You hear our prayers. We want to tell You about. . . .** Briefly pause for children to pray silently. Then say, **Now we'll be quiet so that we can hear Your voice. Help us know the right things You want us to do.** Briefly pause. End the prayer time by saying, **Thank You for Your love. In Jesus' name, amen.**

Getting Crafty
Musical Chimes

What Each Child Needs

16 ounce plastic cup

permanent marker

hole punch

scissors

ribbon

9 or more jingle bells in various sizes

fishing line

What Each Child Does

1. Turn your cup upside down and write "Listen to God" on the side of the cup. Punch three evenly spaced holes around and just below the lip of the cup,

2. With an adult's help, use sharp scissors to carefully make two small holes in the bottom of the cup. Thread an 8- to 10-inch (20.5 to 25.5-cm) piece of ribbon through holes and tie ends together to make a hanger.

3. Tie three or more jingle bells onto an 18-inch (45.5-cm) piece of fishing line, spacing out the jingle bells on the line. Tie end of the line to the cup through one of the holes in the cup. (Hint: Ask a friend to hold up your cup while you attach the fishing line.) Repeat step two more times so that you have three lines of bells attached to your cup.

4. At home, hang your chimes somewhere where you will hear them. Every time you hear the sound of your chimes, let it be a reminder to listen to God.

Getting Active

What You Need

Bible

large sheet of paper

marker

masking tape

What You Do

1. **We can be ready to listen to God when He speaks. Let's play a game where we practice listening.** Print 1 Samuel 3:10 on a large sheet of paper. Display paper in your playing area.

2. Children form two equal teams. Whisper a number to each child on each team (for example, whisper the numbers one through eight if there are eight children on the team). Do not whisper the numbers in order.

3. Children walk around the playing area and clap the number you whispered to them. They may not talk to each other; they must listen to the number of claps to figure out what number each child was given. Children line up in their teams in numerical order.

4. The first team to line up correctly says 1 Samuel 3:10 in order, each child saying one word at a time, referring to the paper as needed.

5. Begin a new round of the game, whispering a different number to each child. Children play again as above.

Faith Builders at Home

Parents: Use these ideas to help build your child's faith, encouraging your child to become a lifelong follower of Jesus Christ.

> "Then Samuel said, 'Speak, for your servant is listening.'"
> 1 Samuel 3:10
>
> ## Key Word
>
> **Listen: To pay attention to what someone says.**

Fun at Home

Ask your family to work together to think of several slogans encouraging people to listen to God's voice. For ideas, read Proverbs 1:8 and James 1:22, or rewrite a familiar commercial. Letter the slogans in some form of decorative writing (using a variety of colored markers, in block letters, etc.) on a strip of paper. Display the slogans on a wall.

Quick Pick

Play a coin-toss game. Take turns tossing a coin into the air. If it lands tails-up, each person says the words of 1 Samuel 3:10, substituting his or her name for Samuel's name. If it lands heads-up, each person tells something right to do God has said in His Word, the Bible.

Steppin' Out

One of the ways we hear God speak to us is through worship services at church. Help your child enjoy positive experiences at church by following these guidelines: (1) Sit toward the front of your church sanctuary so that your child can see and fully participate. (2) Before or after a song is sung, define any unfamiliar words. (3) Bring a Bible, and when Scripture is read, help your child follow along in the Bible. (4) Before or after the worship service, be sure to introduce your child to at least one other adult.

The Reason for the Season (Christmas)

Lesson 48
Nothing Is Impossible

"For nothing is impossible with God."
Luke 1:37

Key Word

Miracle: Something only God can do.

Opening Up

What do you think the word "impossible" means? What is something that is impossible to do? Invite children to tell ideas.

Checking Out God's Word

We can think of a lot of things that are impossible for us to do. But the Bible tells us that God can do miracles—things that are impossible for anyone else to do. Let's read about some miracles that God did. Have a child read Luke 1:26-33 aloud.

■ **Who did God send to talk to Mary?**

■ **What miracle did the angel say was going to happen to Mary?**

Mary knew that even though she didn't understand how it would happen, she was going to have a baby who would be God's Son, Jesus. In Luke 1:37 the angel told Mary "For nothing is impossible with God."

■ **Do you think Mary believed the angel? Why or not?**

■ **Read Luke 1:38 to see what Mary told the angel. What do her words show about what she believed?**

Sometimes we might think that it's impossible for God to help us or hear our prayers. Sometimes we might think it's impossible for God to forgive our sins. But we can remember that God can do miracles—even sending His Son Jesus to be born!

Talking to God

Today as we pray, let's remember that God can answer our prayers, even things we might think are impossible! Invite children to tell their prayer requests and then lead children in prayer. **Dear God, thank You for sending Jesus to be born. Thank You for all the great and wonderful things You do. In Jesus' name, amen.**

Getting Crafty
Christmas Wreath

What Each Child Needs

two 9-inch (23-cm) paper plates

scissors

green paint

paintbrush

marker

stapler

hole punch

8-inch (20.5-cm) piece of ribbon
(any color)

glue

10 to 15 individually wrapped
candies

optional—green paper plates with
green front and back

What Each Child Does

1. (Optional: Use green paper plates with green front and back.) Fold one plate in half. Cut a circle out of the middle of the plate. Make sure you leave an outside rim big enough to glue candies on. Paint the bottom side of this plate green. Set aside to dry.

2. On the other plate, write the words of Luke 1:37 in the center of the plate.

3. Place the plates together with the tops facing each other. Staple plates together along the outer rims. Punch a hole at the top of the plates. Tie a ribbon through the hole to use as a hanger.

4. Lay the plates flat with the painted side up. Glue candies around the edge of the plate. Let it dry completely before hanging up. (Optional: Count the number of days left until Christmas. Glue that number of candies on the wreath. Every day take off one candy.)

Getting Active

| Luke 1:37 | For | nothing | is impossible | with | God. |

What You Need

Bible

large sheet of paper

marker

index cards (six for each child)

pencils

optional—Christmas stickers

What You Do

1. Print Luke 1:37 on a large sheet of paper, drawing lines between each word.

2. Give each child six index cards. Children copy verse onto cards, dividing verse as shown (see sketch). (Optional: Children decorate cards with Christmas stickers.) Collect all cards and shuffle them together.

3. Lead children in playing a game similar to Go Fish. Place all cards facedown in a pile. Each child takes a turn to choose six cards. Children look at their cards to see what they need in order to complete the verse. First player asks any child for a card he or she needs. If a child has the card, he or she must give the card to the player, ending the first player's turn. If a child doesn't have the card, the first player chooses a card from the pile. Play continues until one child has collected all of the words to Luke 1:37 and places the cards in order face up on table or floor. Winner reads verse aloud.

Faith Builders at Home

Parents: Use these ideas to help build your child's faith, encouraging your child to become a lifelong follower of Jesus Christ.

"For nothing is impossible with God."
Luke 1:37

Key Word

Miracle: Something only God can do.

Steppin' Out

Make some sugar cookies together, using Christmas shape cookie cutters. As you decorate and then eat the cookies, see how many miracles you can name that were part of the story of Jesus' birth (angel visits Mary, angels tell good news to shepherds, star leads wise men to Bethlehem, angel warns Joseph in a dream of King Herod's plan to kill baby Jesus, etc.).

Quick Pick

Think of someone (family member, neighbor, relative, friend) who is facing a difficult time. Pray together for the person, asking for God's help in this impossible situation.

Fun at Home

List as many phrases as you can that describe miracles God has done (created the world, forgives sin, answers prayers, sent Jesus, gives us courage, etc.). Then one person writes one phrase in the center of a large sheet of paper. Each person takes a turn to add another phrase, connecting it to the first phrase. See if you can connect all the phrases on your list.

The Reason for the Season (Christmas)

Lesson 49
Room for Jesus

"Let us fix our eyes on Jesus, the author and perfecter of our faith."
Hebrews 12:2

Key Word

Focus: To look in a certain direction without being distracted.

Opening Up

When might a kid your age feel left out or forgotten about? How would you feel if that situation happened to you? Invite children to respond.

Checking Out God's Word

None of us like feeling left out or forgotten. But that's exactly what happened to Jesus. The Bible tells us about a time when Jesus, God's own Son, was left out. Let's read and find out what happened. Have a child read Luke 2:1-7 aloud.

■ Why did Joseph and Mary travel to Bethlehem?

■ Where did Mary give birth to baby Jesus? Why?

■ Imagine that you were an innkeeper in Bethlehem. How might you have felt when you told Mary and Joseph that there was no room for them in your inn?

■ What did the innkeeper miss out on by sending them away?

Because Christmas is an exciting time with gifts, decorations and parties, we sometimes act like the innkeeper when we forget that Jesus' birth is the reason we celebrate Christmas. Even though Christmas is a fun and exciting holiday, we can focus our attention on the real reason we love Christmas. Read Hebrews 12:2 aloud.

Talking to God

(Optional: Complete craft activity before this section. Have children say prayer while holding unlit candle.) **Today let's thank God for sending Jesus so we can know and experience His love and forgiveness.** Help children form a circle. Have children whisper the following prayer to each other one at a time: "We thank God for sending Jesus." Begin the prayer yourself, whispering the prayer to the child next to you. After the prayer has been said around the circle, end the prayer time by asking God's help to stay focused on Jesus during Christmas.

Getting Crafty

Christmas Candle

What Each Child Needs

newspaper

4-inch (10-cm) clay saucer

acrylic paint in assorted Christmas colors

paintbrushes

3-inch (7.5-cm) pillar candle

Christmas stickers

letter stickers

optional—various sizes of candles and
   saucers

What Each Child Does

1. Spread newspaper over your work area. Paint the clay saucer with one color and set it aside to dry. (Optional: If you have provided candles and saucers in a variety of sizes, help each child choose a candle and saucer that fit together.)

2. Decorate candle with stickers. Consider spelling a message on the candle like "Jesus is the Reason."

3. Use other paint colors to paint details on the saucer. After saucer is dry (about 15 minutes), place the candle in the saucer.

4. Take your candle home and place on your dinner table. With your mom or dad, light the candle as a reminder that Jesus is our focus at Christmas. (Optional: Make an extra candle to give as a Christmas gift to someone special.)

Getting Active

What You Need

masking tape
three large sheets of butcher paper
two lengths of yarn
3x5-inch (7.5x12.5-cm) pieces of red and green construction paper
markers
two rolls of transparent tape

What You Do

1. Make a masking-tape line on one side of the playing area. Roll up two of the sheets of butcher paper to make two scrolls and tie with yarn. (Optional: Use a rubber band to tie scrolls.)

2. Invite children to list as many ways to celebrate Jesus' birth as they can (singing Christmas carols, decorating, making cookies, sending Christmas cards). List ideas on remaining sheet of butcher paper. Each child writes one idea from the list on a piece of red or green paper.

3. Divide class into two teams. (Children keep their own pieces of paper.) Teams line up behind masking-tape line. Place one scroll and roll of tape opposite each team on the other side of the room. At your signal, first player on each team runs with his or her piece of paper to a scroll, unties and unrolls it, then tapes the paper onto the scroll before rolling it back up and tying it again. Continue until all players have completed the relay.

4. Two volunteers from the winning team unroll the team's scroll and hold scroll open for others to read. One at a time, read aloud the ways of celebrating Jesus' birth attached to the scroll. Two volunteers from the other team unroll the scroll and hold it open to see if there are any additional ways of celebrating Christmas mentioned. Encourage children to write additional items on the scroll.

Faith Builders at Home

Parents: Use these ideas to help build your child's faith, encouraging your child to become a lifelong follower of Jesus Christ.

> "Let us fix our eyes on Jesus, the author and perfecter of our faith."
> Hebrews 12:2
>
> ## Key Word
>
> **Focus: To look in a certain direction without being distracted.**

Quick Pick

Act out the words to a familiar Christmas carol such as "Away in a Manger" or "Silent Night."

Steppin' Out

Have a memory contest as a reminder that Jesus is the reason we celebrate Christmas. Collect items that picture or symbolize the story of Jesus' birth (one or two Christmas cards, ornaments, nativity scene figures, cookie cutters, etc.). Place all items on a tray. Family members look at items for 10 seconds. Then cover the items with a cloth or towel. See how many items you can remember. Repeat several times, extending the time family members look at items by 10 seconds.

Fun at Home

Pair up family members and have a staring contest. The winner recites Hebrews 12:2 and tells one way he or she can focus on Jesus this Christmas.

The Reason for the Season (Christmas)

Lesson 50
Heard the Good News?

"I bring you good news of great joy that will be for all the people."
Luke 2:10

Key Word

Good News: The news about Jesus' birth.

Opening Up

When have you ever given someone good news? When has someone told you some good news? What was the news? Why was the news so good? What did you do when you heard the news? Invite children to respond.

Checking Out God's Word

When Jesus God's Son and the promised Savior for all people was born, it was good news for everyone! We have heard this good news by reading it in the Bible, or by having someone tell us the news. But one group of people heard this good news in an incredible way! The story is found in Luke 2:8-20. Have a child read Luke 2:8-20 aloud.

■ **Who heard the good news? How was the good news given?**

■ **What did the shepherds do after hearing the good news?**

■ **What did the shepherds do after seeing baby Jesus?**

When we hear exciting news, we usually can't wait to tell someone else! The Bible says that the shepherds "spread the word concerning what had been told about this child" (Luke 2:17).

■ **Why do you think the shepherds shared everything they knew about Jesus?**

Because we know the good news about Jesus, we can be excited to tell about Him, too!

Talking to God

Let's think about how we can tell others the good news about Jesus' birth. Pair up children and give each pair a pencil and sheet of paper. **With your partner, write as many places you can think of where you can tell others the good news about Jesus' birth.** Allow children time to write ideas. **Choose one place on your list to finish today's prayer.** Lead children in prayer. **Father God, thank You for giving us Jesus. Help us to tell others the good news about Jesus at (basketball practice). In Jesus' name, amen.**

Getting Crafty
Good News Angel

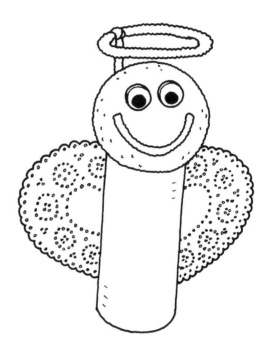

What Each Child Needs

toilet paper tube

white craft paint

paintbrush

yellow or gold chenille wire

red chenille wire

3-inch (7.5-cm) styrofoam ball

scissors

craft glue

two ¹/₄-inch (.6-cm) wiggly eyes

two small white heart doilies

What Each Child Does

1. Paint toilet paper tube white. Set aside to dry.

2. Use the yellow or gold chenille wire to form a small halo. Leave a 1¹/₂-inch (4-cm) end on the halo. Trim off any excess chenille wire. Push the end of the halo into the styrofoam ball so the halo appears to float above the ball.

3. With an adult's help, cut a 1¹/₂ inch (4-cm) piece of red chenille wire. Bend wire to form a smile. Push ends of chenille wire into the styrofoam ball and bend the smile shape to lay flat against the ball. Glue wiggly eyes in place on ball.

4. Spread craft glue on one side of toilet paper tube. Glue one of the heart doilies to toilet paper tube. Spread more glue over doily and overlap second doily. The hearts should extend beyond each side of toilet paper tube to form wings.

5. Spread craft glue around top edge of the tube. Place styrofoam ball firmly on top and allow it to dry completely. (Optional: Use angel as a Christmas tree topper to remind you that the angels told the good news about Jesus at the first Christmas.)

Getting Active

What You Need

one shepherd costume (towels, bathrobes, fabric lengths, sandals, walking sticks, etc.)
  for each group of six to eight children
large paper bags

What You Do

1. Place the materials for each costume in a separate paper bag at one end of an open playing area.

2. Using materials from one paper bag, demonstrate how to dress as a shepherd. When you are completely dressed up, hold the walking stick and call out, "Jesus the Savior is born today!" Return the materials to bag.

3. Children form teams of no more than six to eight. Teams stand in single-file lines across the playing area from paper bags. At your signal, the first child on each team runs to his or her team's bag, dresses up in shepherd clothes, holds up the walking stick and calls out, "Jesus the Savior is born today!" Child puts clothes back in bag and returns to his or her team. The next child in line repeats the action. Children continue taking turns until all children have had a turn. Play again as time allows.

Faith Builders at Home

Parents: Use these ideas to help build your child's faith, encouraging your child to become a lifelong follower of Jesus Christ.

"I bring you good news of great joy that will be for all the people."
Luke 2:10

Key Word

Good News: The news about Jesus' birth.

Fun at Home

Make Christmas pancakes by using red or green food coloring in pancake batter. Buy various colors of cake decorating gel to write on cooled pancakes messages celebrating Jesus' birth.

Steppin' Out

Have your child help you choose a nativity scene to purchase. Set up the nativity scene in your home or front yard for the Christmas season. (Optional: Take a walk or drive through your neighborhood and look at outdoor nativity scenes.)

Quick Pick

Give each family member markers and a sheet of paper. Create a newspaper headline to tell others the good news about Jesus' birth: "Special Child Born Today!" or "Mysterious Light in Sky." (Optional: Write the headlines in big letters directly onto a newspaper page.)

The Reason for the Season (Christmas)

Lesson 51
God's Gift to Us

> "Thanks be to God for his indescribable gift!" 2 Corinthians 9:15

Key Word

**Gift: Something given to someone else without
expecting to be paid back.**

Opening Up

**What is one of the best gifts you've
ever been given? Why was the gift so
special to you? What did you say or
do when you received it?** Invite children to respond.

Checking Out God's Word

**Giving and receiving gifts is a fun part
of Christmas! When we give a gift, we
give it without expecting to be paid
back. That's what God did at the first
Christmas when He sent Jesus to be
born.** Read Luke 2:1-20 aloud. (Optional:
Children tell this familiar story as a
group, one sentence at a time. Begin by
saying "Joseph and Mary traveled to
Bethlehem." A child who volunteers says
a sentence that tells the next event in the
story: "Bethlehem was very crowded."
Continue until the story is complete.)

**The greatest gift we've ever received
is Jesus, because Jesus' life, death and
resurrection made it possible for us
to become members of God's family!
There is nothing we can do to pay
God back for such an incredible gift.**

■ **How might you show your thanks
when you have received a gift you
really like?**

■ **How did the shepherds thank God
for sending Jesus in verse 20?**

■ **What can you do to show your
thanks for Jesus?**

**Just like the shepherds praised and
thanked God, we can celebrate God's
gift to us too—Jesus!** Read 2 Corinthians 9:15 aloud.

Talking to God

Collect a small soft ball. Children sit in a
circle. Give the ball to the child whose
birthday is closest to Christmas. **Today
we're going to thank God for Jesus and
for the many other gifts He's given us.
When the ball is rolled or tossed to
you, complete this sentence: Thank
You, God, for the gift of. . . ."** Hold the
ball and begin the prayer yourself. Roll
or toss the ball to a child in the circle.
Continue prayer until all children have
had the opportunity to participate.
(Note: If a child does not wish to pray,
he or she simply rolls or tosses the ball
to another child.)

Getting Crafty
The Greatest Gift

What Each Child Needs

markers

1-inch (2.5-cm) wooden bead

large empty matchbox

Easter grass or raffia

4-inch (10-cm) square of white fabric

wrapping paper

scissors

craft glue

bows or ribbons

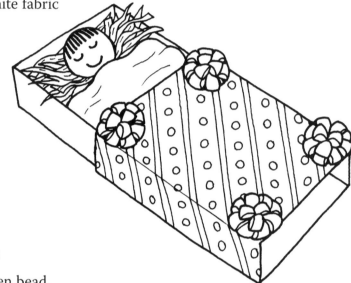

What Each Child Does

1. Draw a face on the wooden bead.

2. Slide off outside portion of matchbox. Fill matchbox with Easter grass or raffia. Tuck the white fabric in and around the sides of the matchbox to look like a blanket.

3. Glue the wooden bead at the top edge of the blanket to represent the face of baby Jesus. Slide back on the outside portion of the matchbox.

4. Cut a piece of wrapping paper the same width as the box. Make sure paper is long enough to wrap around matchbox. Glue wrapping paper around the matchbox. Do not glue wrapping paper around ends of matchbox. (Matchbox must be able to open and close.) Add ribbons or bows for decoration.

5. Keep your project under your Christmas tree as a reminder that the greatest gift to us is Jesus!

Getting Active

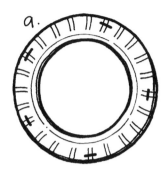

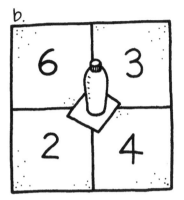

What You Need

paper plates

scissors

measuring stick

stapler

3 foot (.9 m) square of butcher paper

marker

small plastic water bottle (filled with water)

scratch paper

pencils

What You Do

1. Cut the center section out of two paper plates, leaving at least a ring 1-inch (2.5-cm) wide. Staple the plates together, one on top of the other, to create a sturdy ring (see sketch a). On butcher paper square, draw and number sections and place water bottle as shown in sketch b.

2. Children line up approximately 4 feet (1.2 m) from prepared paper. Give the paper-plate ring to the first child in line.

3. At your signal, the first child tosses the ring at the bottle. Child determines points based on where ring lands, retrieves ring and gives it to the next child in line. (Note: A ring that circles the bottle scores 10 points.) Next child repeats action. Children keep track of points on scratch paper. Child with the highest score when you call "stop" tells one reason why Jesus is a special gift to the world. Repeat play as time allows.

Faith Builders at Home

Parents: Use these ideas to help build your child's faith, encouraging your child to become a lifelong follower of Jesus Christ.

"Thanks be to God for his indescribable gift!" 2 Corinthians 9:15

Key Word

Gift: Something given to someone else without expecting to be paid back.

Steppin' Out

With your family, collect and assemble a Christmas kit that can be given to a homeless shelter for children. In a Christmas gift bag, put items such as a package of Christmas stickers, a children's book about the first Christmas, Christmas cards along with envelopes and stamps, Christmas cookies, etc.

Fun at Home

Videotape your family as you take turns reading or telling parts of the Christmas story and/or singing carols. Send the tape as a gift to someone you love who is far away. (Keep a copy as a special family memory!)

Quick Pick

Read the Christmas story from Luke 2:1-20, and then read one or more contemporary Christmas storybooks. As a family, evaluate the contemporary books by identifying which parts of the story match the biblical version.

The Reason for the Season (Christmas)

Lesson 52
Our Gift to God

> "Love the Lord your God with all your heart and with all your soul and with all your strength." Deuteronomy 6:5
>
> ### Key Word
>
> Promise: To say you will do something.

Opening Up

What were some of the best gifts you gave to others this Christmas? What made these such good gifts? How did the people act when they opened your gifts to them? Invite children to respond.

Checking Out God's Word

When we give someone a gift, it's fun to see how much the person likes the gift and to hear the person say thank you. The Bible tells the story of some people who were so glad for the gift of Jesus that they gave gifts in return! Let's find out what happened. Have a student read Matthew 2:1-12 aloud. (Optional: Children pantomime the actions of this story as a narrator briefly tells the story.)

- Why do you think the wise men looked for so long and traveled so far to find Jesus?

- Why do you think they brought Him gifts?

The wise men showed their love and thanks to God for sending Jesus by giving Jesus gifts. We can give God a gift to show our love and thanks to Him, too. Our gift can be a promise to love and obey Him every day. Have a child read Deuteronomy 6:5 aloud.

- What is a way kids your age can show love to God at church? At home?

- What is an example of a way someone your age can obey God?

Talking to God

Let's pray to God and thank Him for His special gift to us—Jesus. Let's also pray and tell God our promise to love and obey Him. Lead children in prayer. Dear God, thank You for sending Your Son, Jesus, to Earth. We love You and we promise to obey You. Please help us do what is right. In Jesus' name, amen.

Getting Crafty
Calendars

What Each Child Needs

12 blank monthly calendar pages for each child

current year calendar

scissors

markers

8¹/₂ x 11-inch (21.5x28-cm) sheet of white cardstock

stapler

optional—print blank calendar pages from the Internet

What Each Child Does

1. Write the 12 months of the year in the top section of separate calendar pages. Using a current year calendar, fill in the dates in the squares for each month.

2. Staple the month pages in order on the bottom half of white cardstock. Make sure to staple only the top edge of the calendar pages so they can be torn off as each month passes.

3. On the top portion of the cardstock, use markers to write Deuteronomy 6:5. Decorate with markers.

4. Use your calendar to help you remember your promise to love and obey God.

Getting Active

What You Need

balloons

garbage bag

chairs

What You Do

1. Inflate one balloon for every pair of children, plus several extras. Transport inflated balloons to playing area in garbage bag. Place several chairs about 3 feet (.9 m) from the edge of one side of the playing area, making sure chairs are at least 4 feet (1.2 m) from each other and that there are approximately two chairs for every eight children.

2. Children form pairs. Give each pair a balloon. Children in pairs decide the best way to hold balloon between themselves without touching it with their hands (between hips, between upper arms, between back and stomach). Pairs practice moving around room in a manner chosen.

3. Invite pairs to stand opposite chairs. Pairs position balloon in manner chosen. At your signal, all pairs move toward chairs, walk around one chair and return to starting position without dropping balloons. First pair back to the starting side names one way to love and obey God. Repeat as time allows.

Faith Builders at Home

Parents: Use these ideas to help build your child's faith, encouraging your child to become a lifelong follower of Jesus Christ.

"Love the Lord your God with all your heart and with all your soul and with all your strength." Deuteronomy 6:5

Key Word

Promise: To say you will do something.

Quick Pick

Talk with your child about a promise you made in the past (marriage, college, career, etc.). Explain to your child why you made the promise and talk about the importance of keeping promises to each other and to God.

Fun at Home

Cut a variety of colored paper or wrapping paper into geometric shapes (squares, circles, triangles, rectangles). On black or white paper, glue the shapes to make pictures of ways to show love and obedience to God.

Steppin' Out

Have your family promise to do something together this week (wash the car, go bowling, see a movie, etc.).

Scripture Index

Scripture Index (continued)

More Great Resources from Gospel Light

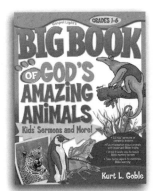

The Big Book of God's Amazing Animals
This book includes 52 lessons about a variety of animals that will intrigue kids, such as dolphins, penguins, koala bears, whales and condors. Each lesson relates facts about the featured animal to a particular Bible verse. As kids learn about fascinating animals that God created, they'll also learn about Him and how He wants them to live.
ISBN 08307.37146

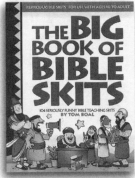

The Big Book of Bible Skits
Tom Boal
104 seriously funny Bible-teaching skits. Each skit comes with Bible background, performance tips, prop suggestions, discussion questions and more. Ages 10 to adult. Reproducible.
ISBN 08307.19164

The Really Big Book of Kids' Sermons and Object Talks with CD-ROM
This reproducible resource for children's pastors is packed with 156 sermons (one a week for three years) that are organized by topics such as friendship, prayer, salvation and more. Each sermon includes an object talk using a household object, discussion questions, prayer and optional information for older children. Reproducible.
ISBN 08307.36573

The Big Book of Volunteer Appreciation Ideas
Joyce Tepfer
This reproducible book is packed with 100 great thank-you ideas for teachers, volunteers and helpers in any children's ministry program. An invaluable resource for showing your gratitude!
ISBN 08307.33094

The Big Book of Christian Growth
Discipling made easy! 306 discussion cards based on Bible passages, and 75 games and activities for preteens. Reproducible.
ISBN 08307.25865

The Big Book of Bible Skills
Active games that teach a variety of Bible skills (book order, major divisions of the Bible, location references, key themes). Ages 8 to 12. Reproducible.
ISBN 08307.23463

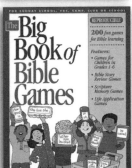

The Big Book of Bible Games
200 fun, active games to review Bible stories and verses and to apply Bible truths to everyday life. For ages 6 to 12. Reproducible.
ISBN 08307.18214

The Big Book of Bible Games #2
150 active games—balloon games, creative team relays, human bowling, and more—that combine physical activity with Bible learning. Games are arranged by Bible theme and include discussion questions. For grades 1 to 6. Reproducible.
ISBN 08307.30532

To order, visit your local Christian bookstore or www.gospellight.com

Gospel Light
God's Word for a Kid's World!

Honor Your
Sunday School Teachers

**On Sunday School Teacher Appreciation Day
the Third Sunday in October**

SUNDAY SCHOOL
TEACHER
APPRECIATION DAY
Third Sunday in October

Churches across America are invited to set aside the third Sunday in October as a day to honor Sunday School teachers for their dedication, hard work and life-changing impact on their students. That's why Gospel Light launched **Sunday School Teacher Appreciation Day** in 1993, with the goal of honoring the 15 million Sunday School teachers nationwide who dedicate themselves to teaching the Word of God to children, youth and adults.

Visit **www.mysundayschoolteacher.com** to learn great ways to honor your teachers on Sunday School Teacher Appreciation Day and throughout the year.

NOMINATE YOUR TEACHERS
FOR SUNDAY SCHOOL TEACHER
OF THE YEAR!
**Winner Receives a Dream Vacation
to Hawaii!**

An integral part of Sunday School Teacher Appreciation Day is the national search for the **Sunday School Teacher of the Year**. This award was established in honor of Dr. Henrietta Mears— a famous Christian educator who influenced the lives of such well-known and respected Christian leaders as Dr. Billy Graham, Bill and Vonette Bright, Dr. Richard Halverson, and many more.

You can honor your Sunday School teachers by nominating them for this award.
If one of your teachers is selected, he or she will receive **a dream vacation for two to Hawaii,** plus free curriculum, resources and more for your church!

Nominate your teachers online at **www.mysundayschoolteacher.com.**

Sponsored by

Gospel Light

*Helping you honor Sunday School teachers,
the unsung heroes of the faith.*

In Partnership With